Books Don't Have To Be Flat!

Innovative Ways to Publish Students' Writing in Every Curriculum Area

By Kathy Pike and Jean Mumper

SCHOLASTIC
PROFESSIONAL BOOKS

New York • Toronto • London • Auckland • Sydney

Interior design by Carmen R. Sorvillo
Cover design by Jaime Lucero
Interior illustrations by Jean Mumper

ISBN: 0-590-12049-2

Dedication

~~~~~~

To my new friends and colleagues at Cambridge Central School, especially Charlie Noe, Superintendent. Also to Alice and Maria for their friendship and inspiration.

—Kathy Pike

To my colleagues and the many others who have chosen the teaching profession.

—Jean Mumper

Acknowledgements

~~~~~~

Our warmest appreciation to those who helped us transform such *ordinary* materials as cans, boxes, plastic bags, hangers, etc., into a professional resource—our families, our editors at Scholastic, our students, and the many teachers who create *extraordinary* literacy experiences throughout the curriculum.

Table of Contents

Introduction:
Developing Students' Multiple Intelligences

Columbus believed that the world didn't have to be flat. We believe literacy projects don't have to be flat—that is, lifeless, dull, two-dimensional. In fact, book and other literacy projects can be inspiring, colorful, and animated. They can make use of such ordinary items as boxes, plastic and paper bags, and cans!

Many of you may be familiar with the folk tale "Something from Nothing," in which a blanket is transformed into a jacket, vest, handkerchief, button, and finally a story. Well, the activities presented in this book will transform ordinary book reports and other assignments across the curriculum into extraordinary projects. They'll inspire your students and show that you can indeed create "something from nothing," or at least "a lot from a little." At the same time, these tools will provide meaningful literacy experiences that require thinking and critical analysis, as well as creative applications.

The textbook was once the central means of instructional delivery. Consequently, we judged students mostly on their ability to absorb the content, generally through tests or assigned book reports. They received instruction rather than actively participating in their own learning. Now educators realize that students learn best when actively involved—and they have different and preferred learning styles and strengths.

With the concept of Multiple Intelligences came an awareness that students need various learning opportunities. It also showed that learning may best be expressed through a variety of modes and experiences. By now, many of you are familiar with Multiple Intelligences. And you may have already adjusted your curriculum to accommodate the different intelligences your students possess. If you haven't, you may want to review the intelligence types listed below—and think of how they might apply to your students.

Verbal/Linguistic (word smart)

This intelligence relates to the capacity to use words effectively, in both speaking and writing. It includes the ability to manipulate the structure, sounds, and meaning of language, as well as mastering its practical uses. Students gather information from reading textbooks or literature and express their knowledge through language-based means.

Key Question:

"How can students use the spoken word to create and display print?"

Logical/Math (number smart)

Often referred to as scientific thinking, this intelligence involves the capacity to use numbers effectively and reason well. It deals with inductive and deductive reasoning, numbers, and the recognition of abstract patterns. Students enjoy deducing, categorizing, calculating, classifying, and hypothesizing.

Key Question:

"How can students organize their learning?"

Musical/Rhythmical (music smart)

This intelligence involves the capacity to perceive, identify, transform, and express various musical forms. Sensitivity to tonal patterns, rhythm, pitch, melody, and beats underpin this aptitude. It also involves the ability to think in musical terms, hear themes, and produce music. Students prefer to sing and rap and maybe even make up songs.

Key Question:

"How can music be brought into the curriculum, and rhythms of language be highlighted?"

Visual/Spatial (picture smart)

This intelligence relies on the sense of sight and the ability to visualize objects. It entails the capacity to create mental images and represent and manipulate spatial configurations. Those who possess this intelligence prove sensitive to color, line, shape, form, and space. Students flourish in visual thinking, benefiting from resources like films, maps, graphic organizers, and charts.

Key Question:

"How can learning be organized through the use of graphic organizers and reading strategies?"

Bodily/Kinesthetic (body smart)

This intelligence relates to movement and the ability to use all or part of the body to perform tasks or solve problems. Hand-to-eye coordination, agility, and physical expressiveness emerge as clear signs of this aptitude. Students enjoy activities that involve physical movement.

Key Question:

"How can students be helped to set their own goals and improve upon their metacognitive behaviors?"

Interpersonal (people smart)

This intelligence operates through person-to-person relationships. It stems from the ability to understand other individuals and to act productively on the basis of that knowledge. Collaborative work proves fruitful for those with interpersonal skills. Students relate to the sensitivity of others and prefer cooperative-learning and other group activities.

Key Question:

"How can thinking be encouraged through conversations and peer interactions?"

Intrapersonal (self-smart)

This intelligence involves knowledge of one's self, both emotionally and cognitively. It also comprises the capacity to engage in self-reflection and metacognition (thinking about thinking) to guide and understand behavior. Students respond well to independent projects and prefer to work at their own pace.

Key Question:

"How can students use their whole bodies and hands-on experiences to enhance their learning?"

Naturalist (nature smart)

This intelligence includes responsiveness to the environment and a love of the outdoors. It involves the ability to relate to and benefit from one's surrounding space. Ecology and other natural sciences provoke the curiosity and showcase the aptitude of children with this intelligence. Students enjoy activities that involve the outdoors and nature.

Key Question:

"How can the outdoors and the environment be brought into the curriculum?" (Gardner, 1983; Armstrong, 1994)

Can you match an intelligence (or intelligences) with certain students? Although some students will appear to possess a high level of functioning in one or two intelligences, all people have capacities in all eight intelligences. With this book, you can match your students' strengths with meaningful literacy experiences that go beyond the traditional curriculum—and that aren't mere craft activities. You'll also have the opportunity to help students tap into other intelligences as they express their literacy in myriad ways.

Books Don't Have to Be Flat! evolved from many years of successful workshops for both preservice and inservice professionals. It also results from many years of working with school-age students, who were given the opportunity to show what they know in a variety of ways. The enthusiasm and the learning that have occurred affirm the success of the activities proposed in this book.

We've included 10 *Books Don't Have to Be Flat!* activities. The number *10* was chosen to correspond to the months in a traditional school year. However, we haven't set out to present a menu of activities. Instead we want to offer choices for different means of expression. If you focus on one type of literacy extension each month, you won't be overwhelmed— and you'll probably recognize additional opportunities not provided here. With formats that allow and even encourage independence, your students will likewise take off in their own creative and exploratory investigations.

Each activity is organized in a similar fashion: Description, Materials, How to Prepare, Across the Curriculum, and Suggested Literature. Illustrations and photographs demonstrate the activity. To explain how individual activities can be fit into a larger picture, we've included a thematic unit—Children Around the World: A Multicultural Study.

We hope that you will have as much fun as our students, colleagues, and we have had creating literacy experiences. Perhaps this book will enable you to turn "a lot from a little" into a meaningful literacy program for your students. Books don't have to be flat—they can be full of life and inspiration, full of animation and color.

Are you "in a pickle" to come up with ways to teach figurative language? Here's an illustrated baggie book of idioms, compiled after learning about our unique language!

Baggie Books

Description

Baggie books are clear, resealable books made from plastic bags (quart- or gallon-size.) The individual pages, which are bound together with tape, contain the contents of the book. Durable and reusable, baggie books allow you and your students to periodically change the contents of the pages. And the plastic acts as lamination, protecting the text.

Materials

- Clear resealable plastic bags (available at grocery stores)
- Posterboard or index cards
- Paper
- Art materials
- Tape (vinyl, gym, duct, electrical, or masking)
- Pictures (cut from magazines), objects (to glue to pages)

How to Prepare

To start the baggie books, cut pieces of tape to lengths slightly smaller than the width of the bags, one piece per bag. Then tape a single bag directly onto the desk or table surface, with half the width of the tape along the bottom of the bag and the other half adhering to the desk or table. Place a second bag directly on top of the first, laying down another piece of tape to exactly cover the tape on the first bag. Now repeat this process until all the bags are used. After the last page is taped, lift up all the attached bags together. Then carefully fold the tape stack in half over the untaped side of the bottom, creasing it to create a spine for the book. Finally, insert index cards or precut posterboard (slightly smaller than bag) to make the page sleeves firm.

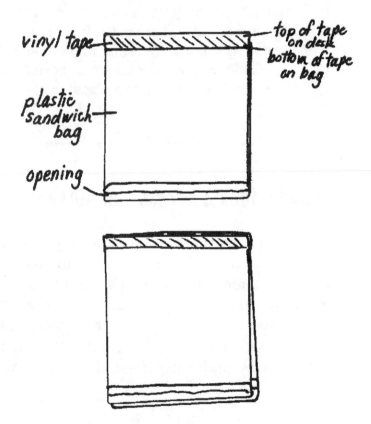

vinyl tape

top of tape on desk
bottom of tape on bag

plastic sandwich bag

opening

Publishing Tip

When buying bags for this activity, it's important to get generic brands, which bear no writing or logos. The "lamination" should be completely clear. To help the book retain its shape, insert precut pieces of cardboard or index cards inside the bags. Once this is done, the book is ready for student work, which is slid into each bag page on top of the posterboard. Both sides of the baggie-book page can be utilized, which increases the number of pages.

To offer a variation of this activity, lay a number of baggies side by side in rows, the number varying according to the desired activity. Then tape them together on the front side. This leaves the bags open in the back, which allows children to insert their work. The connected baggies resemble a quilt that can showcase student-illustrated alphabet books, book jackets, portraits of historical figures, important events, and the like. They can be hung in the class library, in the science or social studies corner, or in any appropriate place in the classroom.

Baggie Books: Across the Curriculum

All areas of the curriculum feature great subjects for baggie books. And, since the plastic sleeves protect the pages, this project works especially well for student-made books that will face repeated handling. Another plus from this activity: Students can take out their wordplay collection (language arts) and put in their annotated flower collections (science). Baggie books make an excellent showcase for students' original writing, illustrations, and collages—and any other work from across the curriculum.

◣ Language Arts

Students can create baggie-book port-folios or baggie-book writing folders by inserting their original writing into the books. Poem collections, essays, and stories work well for this activity. Since baggie books are fun and reward students with a sense of increased pride in their work, they will also enjoy more grammatical tasks like writing and displaying parts of speech or idioms. Here's a brief subject list:

This is a baggie book of Unusual Ways to Use Ordinary Things such as a paper clip, string, and a thumbtack.

- Wordplay (puns, homonyms, palindromes)
- Poetry (original poems, favorite poetry with student illustrations)
- Literary characters (quotations, descriptions, illustrations)
- Elements of stories (setting, characters, problem, events, and resolution)
- Student portfolios
- Parts of speech
- Student writing

◣ Social Studies

Next to language arts, social studies is probably the most content-rich area for the baggie-books activity. Historical figures and events can be depicted for display, as can important documents and primary sources, such as logs, letters, journal entries, and proclamations. The following list suggests some suitable subjects:

- Historical events
- Famous people (portraits and biographies)
- Geographic sites (cities, states, countries, continents)
- Travel logs (postcard collections, brochures, small artifacts)
- Maps (Tip: Students can write on the outside of the baggie with water-based markers that can be erased at a later time.)

- Penny research (Here's a bonus project-within-a-project: A penny minted in a designated year is taped to a card, accompanied by relevant events that occurred during that year.)
- Student research organizer (each bag containing information about an aspect of a topic)

Science

Science illustrates another of the baggie book's advantages: It doesn't have to contain "flat" pages—since objects may be attached to the pages, too. This allows students to display small collections of, for example, flowers, seeds, leaves, or insects. This list will get students writing, examining, and bagging.

Baggie Book of Cloud Poetry: After a study of clouds, students wrote cloud poetry that was placed on cloud shapes against a blue paper background.

- Collections (pressed leaves or flowers; shells, small stones)
- Seasonal changes
- Plant or animal kingdom
- Storms, floods, earthquakes, volcanoes
- Environmental concerns

Math

The baggie-book activity offers an opportunity for students to construct math journals and to document math in everyday occurrences. Students might also display original math games and unique ways to solve mathematical problems. Here's a starter list of bag-able math:

- Number collections and number stories
- Math diaries or journals (solving of problems, reflecting on one's progress)
- Evidence of math in life (timetables, menus, receipts, checks)
- "Math Teasers" book (problems solved and wiped clean on bag)
- Math-game directions (dice, cards, etc., stored in some of the bag-pages)

Suggested Literature

MacLachlan, P. **Sarah, Plain and Tall.**
HarperCollins, 1985. (SS, LA)
Pastoral in its setting and insightful in its
characterization, *Sarah* is a natural for a
social studies or language arts activity. In
fact, there are several ways that students
could utilize baggie books in responding to
this novel. They could compile simulated
letters that Sarah and the other characters
wrote, or they could collect objects (pictures
or student illustrations would do) that per-
tain to the story—like beach sand, paints,
and prairie grass.

Sarah, Plain and Tall: Baggie books are a
perfect way to showcase Sarah's paint-
ings from Maine and the prairie.

Krull, K. **Wish You Were Here: Emily's Guide to the 50 States.**
Doubleday, 1997. (SS, LA)
As a young girl, Emily and her grandmother spend a summer traveling
across the country, and relate the special features and sights of each of
the fifty states. Students may enjoy designing baggie books for their own
states or hometowns—or for any of the other forty-nine states.

Tompert, A. **Grandfather's Tang's Story.** Crown Publishers, 1990. (M, LA)
In this clever little book, Grandfather tells a story using tangrams as
props. Students might enjoy creating their own versions; or they might
write original stories using tangrams as characters. The tangram pieces
could be kept in one baggie so that the book's readers could create the
characters as they read the story.

Ling, M. **Amazing Crocodiles & Reptiles.** Alfred A. Knopf, 1991. (S)
Part of the *Eyewitness Juniors* series, which casts an eye on amazing
behavior in the animal world, this book reports on the habits, diet, and
characteristics of several kinds of crocodiles, alligators, turtles, snakes,
and lizards. It can serve students as an excellent model for further
research on a particular animal. Once their research is concluded, students could complete a baggie book about the chosen animal.

Base, G. **Animalia.** Scholastic Book Club Edition, 1988.
This lavishly illustrated alphabet book challenges the reader to find a myriad of animals beginning with a certain letter. Each illustration is accompanied by a phrase comprised of words that begin with the featured letter. *Animalia* will inspire students to create their own alphabet books. They might also devote an entire baggie book to one letter or tape twenty-six baggies together to make a class alphabet quilt.

Other Suggested Titles

Terban, M. **Too Hot to Hoot: Funny Palindrome Riddles.** Clarion Books, 1985. (LA)
Jordan, M. & T. Jordan. **Amazon Alphabet.** Scholastic, 1996. (S, SS)
Prelutsky, J. **The Random House Book of Poetry for Children.** Random House, 1983. (LA)
Jeunesse, G. **Whales: A First Discovery Book.** Scholastic, 1991. (S)
Locker, T. **Catskill Eagle.** Philomel Books, 1991. (S, SS, LA)

Two students collaborated on a story map for *Tuck Everlasting* by Natalie Babbitt. A road takes the reader on a numbered retelling of significant events in the book.

Story in a Can

Description

Stories in a can (or roll stories) allow teachers and students to illustrate sequential occurrences, plot points, cumulative tales, personal narratives, experiments, and how-to books in a unique format. Beyond offering the means to respond to reading selections and to publish written pieces, this activity lends itself well to other subjects—science, social studies, health and safety, art, and music.

Materials

- Soft-sided cylindrical containers such as those used for potato chips, bread crumbs, oatmeal, nuts, and powdered juice or iced tea (The number will depend on whether the activity is done individually, in small groups, or as a whole class.)
- Adding-machine paper, roll paper, unwaxed butcher paper, mural paper, or sheets of construction or mimeograph paper taped together (Size will vary according to container.)
- Sharp cutting implement for teacher use only (artist knife or single-edged razor blades)
- Crayons, markers, or paints
- Paste or glue
- Self-adhesive paper and felt, fabric, or wallpaper
- Colored tape (optional)

How to Prepare

Prepare the cans by cutting a slit ¼"–½" in diameter, which creates an opening for the finished product to be pulled through. Working with students, cover the can with decorative material. For some children, this (and other steps) will have to be done by an adult or older student. Now cut paper to fit the height of the can (length of paper will vary from can to can). Once you finish these material preparations, choose a curricular area and determine the instructional purpose—for example, showing the various stages in the life of a butterfly.

> **NOTE:** Students can work on their own rolls or on one section of a larger project, which will be attached to classmates' portions when all the contributors have finished. Here's another helpful idea: Some students can work on one sheet of paper at a time; these can later be taped together and onto the roll. This minimizes errors and congestion while working.

Publishing Tip

If possible, laminate the finished product for ease of rolling and for longevity. To help young children identify the beginning of the story, put a piece of colored tape (or draw a colored line) along the edge of the paper. Another piece of different-colored tape can be used to mark the end. Students learn to roll the story from the end by noting the designated color. The tape also strengthens each end of the story.

Story in a Can: Across the Curriculum

All areas of the curriculum can be represented by stories in a can. Naturally, any reading or writing activity that involves description or sequential events can be published using this activity. Specific applications for various areas of the curriculum are listed and described below.

Math

Math phenomena in real life, math operations, word problems, and fractions are but a few of the math elements that can be illustrated and explained using roll stories. Here are a few ways to get students scrolling:

- Fractions
- Story problems
- The 100th day of school
- Calendar (origin, relationship to moon)
- Concepts (more, fewer, greater than, less than)
- Money (counting by twos, fives, tens; making change; foreign currency)
- Math in our lives (advertisements, menus, mileage calculations)
- Math in literature
- Math operations

Language Arts

Writing original stories, depicting events in literature, responding to literature, and illustrating stories or poems are some of the language arts exercises that adapt nicely to the story in a can. These specific activities work well:

- Cumulative stories
- Story grammar (setting, characters, conflict, events, and resolution)
- Retelling wordless stories
- Adaptations of literature (writing a story from the perspective of a character; altering events, characters, or the setting in a story)
- Writing process (research, organization, prewriting, drafting, peer-editing, revision, evaluation, publishing)
- Student self-portraits (timeline of a student's life)
- Learning a new skill (instructions or directions on how to use the computer, how to play an instrument, how to play a game)

Character Timeline:
This roll story shows the major events in Sarah's life in the novel by Patricia MacLachlan.

Autobiographical Timeline:
A fifth grader made this timeline of her life. She chose photographs that signified important events.

Social Studies

Unfolding events, linear descriptions, and progressions or directions frequently crop up in social studies. Depicting the lives of famous people, tracking how a bill becomes a law, tracing the path of an explorer, visiting a foreign country, and showing celebrations around the world are among the subjects that can be portrayed using the story-in-a-can activity. Here are a few specific areas that may be helpful:

- Biographies (Abraham Lincoln, Martin Luther King)
- Timelines (the birth of a nation)
- Family experiences (trips, heritage, celebrations)
- Unfolding historical events (Civil War, colonizing of the New World)
- Transportation (airplanes, cars, trucks, space travel)
- Holidays (Memorial Day, Thanksgiving)
- Photo essays (momentous events, classroom activities, biographies)

Story in a Can: Alphabet Book on a Social Studies Topic (Construction).
(at left) For a unit on construction (complementing the building of a new school wing) students constructed a story-in-a-can alphabet book with key facts and information about construction—architects, blueprints, bulldozers, workers, etc.

Story in a Can: Instructions and Biography. Roll stories can be used to provide instructions on how to make or do something, as in the top project at right. Here, a student has described how to assemble and play a clarinet. In the project shown at bottom, Eleanor Roosevelt is described through significant events in her life.

🍂 Science

Because science includes descriptions of events, phenomena, experiments, cyclical occurrences, and sequential concepts, it offers many areas readily adaptable for the story in a can.

- Experiments (how to make an electrical circuit, ingredients plants need to grow, how liquid becomes a gas)
- Observations (incubation, plant growth, deciduous trees through the seasons)
- Life cycles (caterpillar, frog, humans, food chain)
- Water cycle (saturation→rainfall→evaporation)
- Health (the human body, how to avoid germs)
- Safety (stranger danger, fire prevention, bicycle safety)
- Photo essays of scientific phenomena (the birth of a chick, the changing seasons, a day in the life of a geologist)

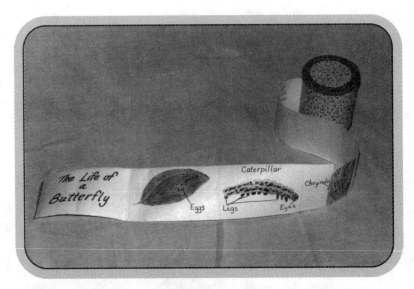

Story in a Can: Life-Cycle Stages. This roll story depicts the stages in the metamorphosis of a butterfly. It was created after a unit of study in science.

Suggested Literature

MacLachlan, P. **Sarah, Plain and Tall.** HarperCollins, 1985. (SS).
Retelling the book is a great way to use the story-in-a-can format.
Students will have fun as they visualize scenes and paste them on mural
paper long enough to accommodate the various depictions from this
image-rich story.

Anno. **Anno's Mysterious Multiplying Jar.** G.P. Putnam's Sons, 1983. (M)
In this book, the number of items on a page multiply as the book is read.
The simple text and captivating pictures introduce the mathematical concept of factorials. Since the progression is linear, your students can write
their own versions for the roll-story format.

Duke, K. **Aunt Isabel Tells a Good One.** Dutton Children's Books, 1992.
(LA)
In a story she makes up to entertain her young niece, Aunt Isabel uses
literary terms like *characters*, *setting*, and *problem.* Students could either
retell the story or write their own versions, paying attention to the elements that comprise stories.

Ling, M. **Amazing Crocodiles and Reptiles.** Alfred A. Knopf, 1991. (S)
Interesting facts and engaging information emerge in this scientific exploration into the world of reptiles. Students might use this creepy-crawly
news, along with other research they may undertake, to report on a particular reptile or amphibian—or they can choose another animal entirely.

Levine, E. **If You Traveled West in a Covered Wagon.** Scholastic, 1986.
(SS)
Using this question-and-answer book about the exploration of the
American West, students can portray the information they've gathered
using the same technique the author used or depict it as a timeline of the
settling of the West. They could also research another area of history and
report on it using a question-and-answer roll story.

Other Suggested Titles

Cushman, K. **The Ballad of Lucy Whipple.** Clarion Books, 1996. (SS)

Lobel, A. **Fables.** Scholastic, 1980. (LA)

Hartman, G. **As the Crow Flies: A First Book of Maps.** Macmillan, 1991.
     (SS, M)

Cole, J. & B. Deegan. **The Magic School Bus Inside the Human Body.**
     Scholastic, 1989. (S, LA)

Ferris, J. **Walking the Road to Freedom: A Story About Sojourner Truth.**
     Carolrhoda/Lerner, 1988. (SS)

Artifact-Box Book: In response to *Sarah, Plain and Tall*, objects were collected or created to reflect both the book and the historical period of its setting, the late 1800s. Items included in this artifact-box book are: a quill, handmade soap, a tintype photograph, a lace handkerchief, dried flowers, marbles, and a paintbrush.

Artifact-Box Books

Description

An artifact-box book is a collection of objects pertaining to something general, such as a topic, a theme, or a book. This activity encourages higher-level thinking and the use of visual imagery, as it challenges students to find concrete ways to represent concepts, feelings, and memories—or any other subject that can be represented by using objects as symbols. In order to choose and collect these symbols, students must analyze what they have learned and present it in an alternate way. The choices students make and the rationale they offer can be quite intriguing.

Materials

- Wide assortment of objects
- Containers (bags, boxes, baskets, etc.)
- Art supplies (fabric, felt, markers, paints, glue)
- Paper or index cards

How to Prepare

After reading a book or completing a unit of study, you might highlight some desired aspect of the learning. Students then collect representative objects that illustrate the theme or focus. They are placed in a container—like a bag, a box, a briefcase, a suitcase, or a basket. On paper or index cards, students can identify the artifact items and provide a brief description to show their connection to the topic.

Publishing Tip

Objects can be amassed in creative containers. For example, a box can be decorated to resemble the Magic School Bus for a reading of a book in that popular series. Or a bag can become a rocket ship for a time capsule inspired by a science fiction selection like *The Green Book.* Cigar boxes can also be used. If the artifact-box book is to represent a class member, a character in a book, or an historical figure, your students can decorate the outside of the box with personal or relevant pictures, original artwork, writing, or quotes.

Artifact-Box Books: Across the Curriculum

Collecting objects to symbolize various areas of the curriculum is a motivating and thought-provoking activity. It's also lots of fun. All curricular areas can be enhanced by using artifacts to help create meaning.

Language Arts

Using artifacts will enrich your reading curriculum, as students can represent characters, entire stories, and authors. Artifacts might also be used to represent the students themselves. These personal symbols could then be displayed at Open Houses, Back to School Nights, or in portfolios. Here are a few ideas to get students started on object hunts:

Artifact-Box Book: This is another artifact-box book created for the novel _Sarah, Plain and Tall._

- Self-portraits (important people, events, and interests in students' lives)
- Literature characters (Sarah from _Sarah, Plain and Tall,_ Cinderella)
- Book representations (_The Hundred Box, The Egyptian Cinderella, Johnny Appleseed_)
- Author studies (Jan Brett, Gary Paulsen, Patricia Reilly Giff)
- Capsule of year you (or students) were born

Science

Collections have always proved a fun and informative process in the science curriculum—from fossils to shells to products from certain plants and animals. So artifact representations are no stranger to the budding scientist. And this activity delivers a creative offshoot: Students design lab coats, keeping in mind the kinds of scientists they'll be (for example, geologist, herpetologist, vulcanologist). The coat can be made from white plastic trash bags (with holes for arms), attached to which are items that represent the scientist's life and responsibilities. The items can be pictures from magazines, student illustrations, or even small objects light enough to attach to the trash bag. To begin the year and to get an idea of what students think science is, ask them to bring in items that they think are representative of their field of science—and to justify their choices.

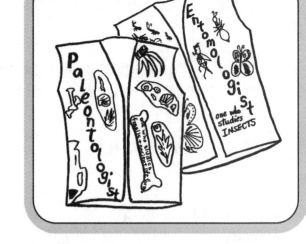

Scientists' lab coats made from white plastic trash bags.

- Products from a natural resource (trees, animals)
- Items representing a biome (the desert, the sea, the mountains)
- Recycled items (various paper, plastic, and rubber products)

Social Studies

Social studies offers many possibilities for artifact representation. Students can use artifacts to describe and flesh out historical events, places around the world, famous people, and time capsules. A brief list follows:

- States or provinces
- Time capsules
- Famous people
- Treasure chests from periods in history
- Historical events (the settling of Plimoth Plantation, the Boston Tea Party, Westward Expansion, the Civil War)
- Countries around the world

Artifact-Box Book: For a Place. This artifact-box book was created using both real objects and student illustrations that reflect Plymouth, Massachusetts. Some of the items included are: sand (in a plastic bag), postcards, candles, cranberry sauce, a lobster claw, and a map. Student research on such things as Massachusetts's state flower, bird, and flag along with its weather and history are also included.

Suggested Literature

MacLachlan, P. **Sarah, Plain and Tall.** HarperCollins, 1985. (SS)
For this classic, young readers could collect things that are representative of the book itself—or of its captivating protagonist Sarah. For example, some objects might include: shells (representing Sarah's seaside origins), letters (Sarah's letters to the children and to her brother), a paintbrush (Sarah's love of painting), and a small toy cat or a picture of a cat.

Fradin, D. **Massachusetts: From Sea to Shining Sea.** Children's Press, 1991. (SS)
An engaging introduction to the state's geography, history, and famous people, this informative book covers the Bay State from Cape Cod to JFK. Students could create an artifact box for the entire state. Their collection might include the state flag, a map, and pictures of John F. Kennedy and John Adams. They could add products associated with the state—cranberries, seafood (clam shells, oyster shells), baked beans—and its famous places (Plimoth Plantation, Harvard University, Cape Cod). For a variation, they could collect items that are representative of a certain city, like Plymouth or Boston. With this activity, information for both the state and the city could be included—for example, a replica of the *Mayflower* or Plymouth Rock, sand to represent beaches, or a bell symbolizing the famous one in Boston's Old North Church.

Mathis, S. **The Hundred Penny Box.** Viking Penguin, 1975. (SS)
In this delightful book, a box contains a penny for each year of Aunt Dew's life. Breathing new life into the saying "a penny for your thoughts," each coin symbolizes a memory that she shares with her great-great nephew. As a response to the literature, students could collect pennies for each year of their own lives, with an accompanying memory or description.

Frasier, D. **On the Day You Were Born.** Harcourt Brace, 1991. (SS)
The richness of history will become apparent to young readers of this fun and thought-provoking book. Students will be inspired to collect items that reflect the year or day of their birth. Collections might include newspapers, popular books or songs, and pictures of athletes or entertainers.

Fox, M. **Wilfred Gordon McDonald Partridge.** Kane/Miller, 1984. (LA, SS) A young boy helps an elderly woman recall her memories by collecting objects that trigger the woman's recollections of her past. Students might amass a collection of objects that are representative of their own memories and describe why each memory has significance. This is an excellent introductory activity for the beginning of the school year or for showcasing students at Parent Open Houses. The memory box does not have to be solely for students; it can represent famous people (from the present or past) or characters in literature. Teachers can likewise use artifact boxes to introduce themselves to their students at the beginning of the year.

Other Suggested Titles

Climo, S. **The Egyptian Cinderella.** HarperCollins, 1989. (LA, SS)
Cole, J. **The Magic School Bus Inside a Hurricane.** Scholastic, 1995. (S)
Walsh, J. **The Green Book.** Farrar, Straus, & Giroux, 1979. (S, LA)
Kellogg, S. **Johnny Appleseed.** William Morrow, 1988. (LA, SS)
Kent, D. **Benjamin Franklin: Extraordinary Patriot.** Scholastic, 1993. (SS)

Pictured here are three versions of graduated-pages books that use colored tabs to indicate the contents. (1). "Colors of Autumn" contains poetry reflecting autumn and the moods evoked by the colors of that season (2). "Hatchet" catalogues and illustrates a literary device used by Gary Paulsen in his novel *Hatchet*. (The author uses color to reflect the feelings of his main character—red for anger, black for despair, and green for hope). (3). "Free Verse Poetry" was inspired by *Hailstones and Halibut Bones* by Mary O'Neill.

Graduated-Pages Books

Description

Doing this activity is not only fun—it gives your students a feel for reference texts. Similar to address books and some thumb-indexed dictionaries or encyclopedias, graduated-pages books allow the reader to locate information readily. They have slightly overlapping pages with a margin at the edge of the pages for tabs, and a label to categorize the information that is recorded on the page. These books do not have to be read sequentially or in their entirety; they can be referred to as needed or desired. And they can be used for any area of the curriculum that has subcategories.

Materials

- Paper
- Markers or other writing materials
- Stapler or tape
- Glue
- Paint chips (paint-color samples), small pictures (see How to Prepare)
- Magazine pictures, photographs, stamps, postcards, and/or students' drawings relating to the chosen topic

How to Prepare

The production of these books and the creation of their content makes for great hands-on small-group projects. And, although paper can be cut to make graduated pages, it isn't necessary to do so. Instead, students can fold paper to make these books. To produce as many pages as needed, use several sheets of legal-size paper. Fold the first sheet, leaving about a ½"–¾" border. Show students a sheet so they can help in the book production. Now, the first sheet is placed on top of a second sheet, which also has a border. Repeat until the desired number of sheets is used. To organize the contents, students can either label the borders or affix pictures or paint chips to them. (If students make books about animals, they might attach a small cut-out picture of a kangaroo to a page featuring marsupials.)

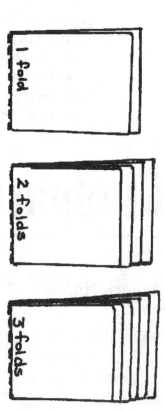

Publishing Tip

In the class writing center, you can keep a variety of materials for making graduated-pages books. Store paint chips (or construction-paper substitutes) in individual envelopes and try to have on hand an assortment of magazine pictures. Having models of books (both student-produced and commercial) constructed in this fashion can provide instruction and inspiration. Also, remember that many companies create brochures using a graduated-pages format, and these could be displayed in the writing center, too.

Graduated-Pages Books: Across the Curriculum

There are many examples of graduated-pages books in real life, from address books to reference texts. Still, homemade graduated-pages books have their place in the school curriculum, too. Broad categories such as "reptiles," "women in history," "Canada," or "the ocean" can be depicted in this manner. Each of the pages in the book can describe a different aspect of the topic. For instance, "Canada" might include a page on customs, on population, on sites of significance, and so on.

Language Arts

There are a variety of literary genres with selections that lend themselves to the graduated-pages format. Here are two literary devices to look for: (1) Color is sometimes used in fiction and poetry to evoke feelings and emotions, to create mood, and to depict setting or atmosphere. A different page (with a corresponding paint-chip tab) can be devoted to each color, with examples from the book or poem(s) written to express the color applied (with paint, pencils, or crayons) to the main part of the page. *Hailstones and Halibut Bones,* a poetry book that presents feelings associated with colors, can be used as a model. On a more abstract level, colors can be associated with characters' moods. For example, in the novel *Hatchet,* a survival tale, red can represent fire and the hope for survival, green can stand for the trees and nature, and black can evoke the darkest moments when Brian, the main character, felt hopeless. (2) Word play is another literary device that works well with this activity. You can use separate examples or categories—like idioms, homonyms, and alliteration—on each graduated page. Here's a list of helpful ideas:

Graduated-Pages Book: Using one aspect of the novel *Sarah, Plain and Tall*—Sarah's life by the sea—this graduated-pages book depicts story events and seaside settings from the book.

- Jokes, riddles, puns
- Address books
- Poems (color poems, student favorites, students' original work)
- Reactions/responses to literature
- Parts of speech (finding examples in literature of nouns, verbs, etc.)
- Phonic elements (finding examples in literature of consonant blends, initial-consonant patterns, etc.)

Math

When exploring number concepts, students enjoy cataloging their findings on graduated pages. They might, for instance, create equations for the number 12, locate examples of mathematics in real life (math in the home, math in fast-food restaurants, math at the mall), or find examples of literature that incorporate math.

A starter list follows.

- Number stories
- Number concepts
- Math in the real world
- Math in literature

Social Studies

Information from social studies proves perfect for display in a tabbed booklet. In fact, a lot of what readers find in published encyclopedias could be classified as social studies information. Examples of topics for which students may compose graduated-pages books are "famous sites in New York State," "rivers around the world," "countries in Europe," "island nations," and "people in history." Here's a list of some graduated-pages book subjects:

- Customs
- Holiday celebrations
- Families
- State histories
- Towns, cities, countries
- Landforms around the world

Science

Since the content of science is classified, it can be easily reported in such a manner. A broad category might serve as a suitable subject for class investigation. Students could then work individually or collectively to locate information for the topics or subcategories. Later, they can share their findings by completing individual pages in the book. The following list offers a few ideas for class investigations:

- Animal and plant kingdoms
- Biomes
- Solar system
- Shapes and colors in nature
- Food pyramid

Suggested Literature

Seuss, Dr. **My Many Colored Days.** Alfred A. Knopf, 1996. (LA)
In this amusing book from the master of fun, various emotions come to life in colors. To create their own emotional hues, students could choose several colors and show how they represent certain moods. For example, red could reflect anger or excitement; green, hope and renewal; and yellow, warmth and caring.

O'Neill, M. **Hailstones and Halibut Bones.** Trumpet, 1961. (LA)
This magical book of poetry offers evocative poems for every color. Each poem can serve as a source of items and emotions representative of its color. As in *My Many Colored Days,* students may choose colors that they feel reflect certain feelings or objects. They could then write poems about the colors, or locate other poems that use color to convey a theme or message, such as *Spring Wears Green Gloves* by Debra Chandre.

Paulsen, G. **Hatchet.** Viking, 1987. (LA, S, SS)
In this compelling tale of survival, the author makes use of colors to help his hero, Brian, cope with the isolation of the wilderness and the divorce of his parents. Red and yellow are used to represent fire (which means survival to Brian), black when Brian reaches his darkest moments, and blue and green to describe the wonders of nature.

Branley, F. **Planets in Our Solar System.** HarperCollins, 1979. (S)
Astronomy comes alive in this simple and informative look at our closest space neighbors. Responding to the book, students can create a mini-encyclopedia of the planets, writing the name of each planet on the graduated-page margin. The body of each page can feature key facts and pictures about the planet of study.

Aliki. **Fossils Tell of Long Ago.** HarperCollins, 1972. (S)
Each page of this innovative book offers information about a particular fossil. Better still, a small picture of the fossil (or its name) appears on the edge of each page for easy reference. So *Fossils* can serve as a model of graduated-pages books. In response, students can use other reference resources to locate additional information about these fossils and to research different fossils. Once they've gathered the information, students can compile a class fossil book.

MacLachlan, P. **Sarah, Plain and Tall.** HarperCollins, 1985. (SS)
One of Sarah's hobbies was drawing, and her life in Maine always brought forth happy memories. Students can combine these aspects of Sarah by constructing a graduated-pages book. Pretending they are Sarah, students will enjoy portraying the seaside in its many colors and trying to capture the varying moods of the ocean. They can label each page with a paint chip and create ocean scenes reminiscent of the chosen colors. For example, on the "green" page, "Sarah" can paint seaweed washing up on the shore or the evergreens that may border the beach.

Other Suggested Titles

Leventhal, D. **What Is Your Language?** Dutton, 1994. (SS)
Kuchalla, S. **What Is a Reptile?** Troll, 1982. (S)
Allen, J. **What Is a Wall, After All?** Candlewick Press, 1993. (SS)
Joose, B. **I Love You the Purplest.** Chronicle Books, 1996. (SS)
Hulme, J. **Sea Squares.** Hyperion Paperbacks for Children, 1991. (M, S)

Children love using boxes in unusual shapes, such as this heart-shaped box with paper cut to fit the form. This book can contain student writing, or poetry on such topics as "I love...," "This makes my heart happy," or "Random acts of kindness."

Box Books

Description

Boxes come in all shapes and sizes. Any box can be used to create box books, from gift boxes to candy boxes to doughnut boxes. Some boxes (such as those in which jewelry is sold) make perfect containers for accordion-style box books, in which the pages are folded in opposing direction, like a paper fan. Deeper boxes with transparent lids, like greeting-card boxes, make excellent window-box books; students' stories are placed inside and viewed through the "window." The beauty of these window-box books is that the order of the stories can be rearranged according to the reader—who may choose to place her or his own contribution on top.

Materials

- Boxes of all sizes and shapes, including some cardboard and transparent plastic lids (If you can't find transparent lids, use overhead transparencies to make windows in cardboard lids.)
- Variety of paper
- Writing/art materials
- Art knife or scissors
- Safety scissors
- Glue or tape
- Fabric or wallpaper

How to Prepare

Collect a variety of boxes to suit your instructional purposes. If the box is to be used to house accordion-style books, paper should be cut to fit inside the box. Students write, draw, or paste on the paper whatever is to be displayed in the books. One or both ends of the paper can be glued to each side of the box. If preferred, the book does not have to be glued at all; instead, it can be read when removed from the box.

If students create window-box books, they can use safety scissors to cut the paper so it fits inside the box. (You can assist with the cutting if some find it too difficult.) Students can draw pictures or paste photos or magazine pictures onto the paper. The books can be sequential, or they can be a collection of pictures, which means they could be read in any order.

Box Books: Across the Curriculum

It's time to box knowledge, share pieces of literature, or present content-area information using this unique format. From retellings of books and original writing samples to timelines and descriptions of scientific phenomena, box stories can contain the information!

Publishing Tip

Since this activity offers two types of box books (accordion-style and window), the front "covers" will vary in appearance. Accordion-style box books allow students to create a more traditional cover with, for example, title, author, and illustration to reflect the contents. This can be glued directly onto the box cover. The window-box book, on the other hand, can be decorated to resemble an actual window—with curtains (made from fabric, wallpaper, or construction paper), flower boxes, and window panes. The first page inside can provide the cover information, or a cover could be pasted onto the back of the box.

Social Studies

Anything sequential or linear can be represented in a box story. Consequently, social studies delivers countless opportunities for this activity. Biographical data, how-to information, the process through which a bill becomes a law, and timelines all prove excellent subjects. Boxes with see-through lids can depict famous sites, battles, and people or customs; holiday celebrations; and children of various cultures.

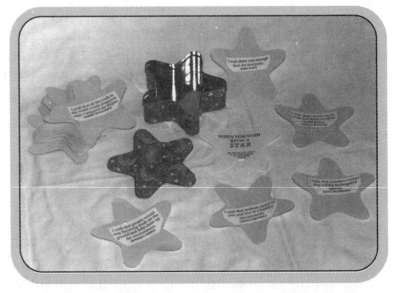

Box Books: A star-shaped box houses student writing on such topics as "I wish...," "Things I do well," and "I'm an All-Star."

Here's the list to get you started:

- Timelines
- Feelings/emotions (Heart-shaped boxes—plentiful in February— might be nice for this topic.)
- Historical events
- Shelters, clothing, and customs from around the world
- Information on cities, states, or countries
- Biographical data of historical figures
- Stamp stories (each page featuring facts on the stamp or its contents)

Language Arts

For many of us, fiction is the first thing that comes to mind when we think of books. Language arts is a great place to start this activity. Stories can be folded, in accordion fashion, to fit into a box, as can poems and other samples of original writing. If students use the window-box approach, they may want their first page to show their knockout illustration work. Whatever they choose, the content of the window-box can vary as widely as that of the accordion-style—for instance, observations of natural phenomena, original poetry with illustrations, stories, and characters in literature are all fair game.

Bedtime Box Book: A cigar box is covered with fabric and transformed into a bed for holding a collection of favorite bedtime stories or poems, a record of dreams and nightmares, a series of essays on fears, or any other work pertaining to sleep or dreams.

A reminder list follows.

- Retelling stories of all genres
- Photo essays
- Class photo gallery
- Original stories, poems, jokes, and riddles

Window-Box Book: Scenes from Sarah's windows in Maine and the Midwest. Window-box books can highlight significant events in a novel.

Science

For science, as for subjects across the curriculum, stories can be accordion-style or window-box. The latter serve as thought-provoking windows into scientific phenomena. Both kinds generate educational fun, and both can depict, for example, cyclical trends, logical processes (like conducting experiments), living organisms, life in the desert, and recycling.

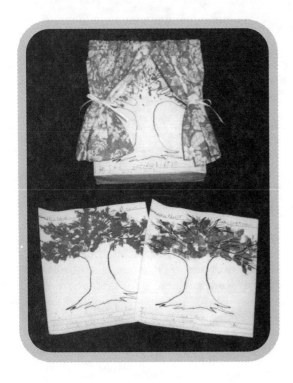

Window-Box Books: Boxes with clear plastic covers are decorated with fabric and lace to create a windowlike effect. These box books contain seasonal poetry (left) and a student's point-of-view essay on what is happening outside the classroom window (above).

The following list of topics might be helpful:

- Weather and seasonal changes
- Solar system
- Animal habitats or biomes
- Plant and/or animal kingdom
- Observations of science experiments; incubation
- Visits to aquariums or science museums
- Destruction or restoration of the environment

◢ Math

"Manipulating " math concepts can be readily accomplished using box books. In "addition," children's literature develops and enhances mathematical reasoning, and these math oriented stories can be retold or illustrated using this *Books Don't Have to Be Flat!* activity.

Accordion-Box Book: A variety of accordion-box books are shown here. They're great for representing information learned during math time: for example, counting, number facts, and number stories.

Some ways that you can "count" on to depict math using box books include:

- Counting
- Number facts
- Math in real life, e.g., menus, graphs and tables, advertisements, schedules
- Story problems
- Comparisons (more, less, greater than)
- Retelling of stories such as *Pigs Will Be Pigs* by Amy Axelrod, *The M&M Counting Book* by Barbara Barbieri, and *How Much Is a Million?* by David Schwartz

Suggested Literature

Cameron, A. **The Most Beautiful Place in the World.** Alfred K. Knopf, 1988. (SS)
This heartfelt book reveals what we all feel in our special connections to places. Although it can be retold in a box book, it might also inspire students to choose and portray their own "Most Beautiful Place in the World." Maybe it's their hometown, a country far away, or a place in their imaginations. Prose pages can be illustrated and placed in window-box books.

DePaola, T. **The Cloud Book.** Holiday House, 1975. (S)
Tomie DePaola introduces the ten most common types of clouds, the myths that have been inspired by cloud shapes, and the hints clouds give us about oncoming weather. In response to this engaging information, both kinds of box-book formats could house portrayals of various clouds or the retelling of a myth. Picture clouds viewed through the panes of a window box! Students' writing and illustrations, magazine pictures, downloaded pictures from the Internet, and weather columns from the newspaper can serve as sources for the box books.

Brenner, B. **If You Were There in 1776.** Macmillan, 1993. (SS)
This interesting treatment of American history demonstrates how the concepts and principles in the Declaration of Independence were drawn from experiences of living in America in the eighteenth century. Brenner places an emphasis on children living on a farm in New England, on a plantation in the South, and on the frontier. Students can create window-

box books to retell these historical episodes, or they might write and illustrate "If You Were There..." accounts.

Selsam, M. **Egg to Chick.** HarperCollins, 1970. (S)
This simple and informative text tracks the fertilization of an egg and the growth and hatching of a chick. Both accordion-style and window-box books can portray the information gleaned from *Egg to Chick.* A classroom incubation study is another great response to this book. If this is undertaken, children can conduct observations through the panes of a window-box book.

MacLachlan, P. **Sarah, Plain and Tall.** HarperCollins, 1985. (SS)
A favorite for most any activity, Sarah delivers again. Using a window-box book, the scenes that Sarah sees can be illustrated and placed in the box. The box book can begin with Sarah's life by the sea in Maine, continue with her trip on the train, and wind down with her relocation to the Midwest.

Baker, J. **The Window.** Viking Penguin, 1991. (S)
This wordless picture book traces the evolution of a wooded land into a city plagued with pollution. It ends on a hopeful note, however, with the introduction of recycling and other attempts to clean up the environment. *The Window* can be used as a springboard to the depiction of environmental scenes, the seasons, animal life in the forest, and so on. Box books might also mirror the "text" by portraying polluted land and showing the stages in its cleanup and revitalization.

Other Suggested Titles

Aliki. **My Visit to the Aquarium.** HarperCollins, 1993. (S)
Aliki. **The Story of Johnny Appleseed.** Trumpet, 1963. (SS)
Weinberg, L. **What Was It Like? Benjamin Franklin.** Longmeadow
    Press, 1988. (SS)
Heller, R. **Many Luscious Lollipops: A Book About Adjectives.** G.P.
    Putnam's Sons, 1989. (LA)
Williams, V. **Stringbean's Trip to the Shining Sea.** Scholastic, 1988. (SS)

Children created Gift Books to give as presents. Some illustrated story events, others chose to showcase their writing.

Gift Books:

Accordion Books with an Added Touch

Description

Gift accordion books take ordinary accordion books and package them in such a fashion that they become perfect gifts. As with traditional accordion books, these books are created from paper folded like a fan. The accordion paper is then attached to two pieces of cardboard and a ribbon. The cardboard, which serves as the front and back covers, may be decorated or covered with fabric or wallpaper. Before attaching the last of the folded pages to the cardboard, ribbon is inserted between the back cover and the last page. Then, when the book is closed, it may be tied and presented to a deserving recipient.

Materials

- Paper, glue and scissors
- Ribbon
- Cardboard, tag board or colored poster board
- Fabric, wallpaper, wrapping paper or colored paper
- Art supplies (markers, paints, colored pencils)

How to Prepare

Along with students, decide on the size and shape of the book and cut the paper accordingly. Fold the pages in a fanlike fashion, taking care to keep each page the same size. Students can write and draw directly on the pages or can paste both illustrations and stories to the pages. The height and width of the book can be increased by taping several folded strips together. The first and last sheets (which may be kept blank if desired) are glued onto decorated cardboard covers. Before gluing the last folded page onto the back cover, insert a piece of ribbon between the two, leaving enough ribbon overhanging to tie around the closed accordion book. Then glue the page onto the cover. Fold the book and tie the ends of the ribbon together across the front cover.

Publishing Tip

It's worthwhile to visit a framing shop for scraps from discarded mat boards—it works perfectly for making the covers of this book. Other types of cardboard, however, will suffice. Wallpaper samples or fabric swatches glued onto the cardboard turn the ordinary into something extraordinary. Although useful throughout the year, gift books make great gifts for that special occasion—holidays, grandparents day, thank-you notes to guest speakers, etc.

Gift Books: Across the Curriculum

When constructing gift books, the pages can be treated as separate wholes or can comprise parts of a story or report. For example, pages can contain samples of poetry, journal entries, or individual character descriptions. They can also tell a story or describe one aspect of a process or category that continues on other pages. Gift books can incorporate desired content area from language arts, social studies, science, art, music, and any other part of the curriculum.

Language Arts

Students can use this format to retell any story, and it also works well for their original stories and poetry. And factual as well as fictional information can be depicted in this manner—for example, journal writing and reports. The gift accordion book is especially well-suited for creating original greeting cards. You can use this list as a jumping-off point.

Gift Book: After reading *Sarah, Plain and Tall*, students can retell the story in a gift book and present it to someone special—grandparents, senior citizens, other family members, friends, etc.

- Character studies
- Literature quotes
- Favorite recipes
- Inspirational sayings
- Photos with captions
- Retelling stories of all genres
- Original stories, poetry, jokes, riddles, recipes
- Greeting cards and thank-you notes
- "Welcome to Our Class" book for an entering student (with information about the school and class)

Social Studies

Since any sequence of events or process can be depicted in a gift book, social studies makes a great curricular base for this activity. Examples of ideal topics include timelines; instructions; biographies; information on cities, states, and countries; customs; holidays; clothing; and geographic phenomena. A short list follows:

- Cultural studies
- Places around the world
- Biographies
- Historical events
- Government processes
  (how laws are made, election of public officials)

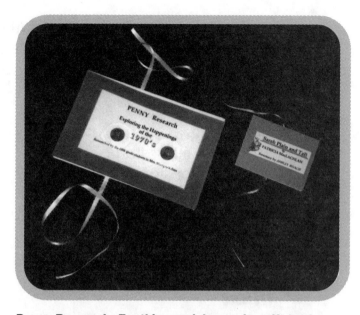

Penny Research: For this special-occasion gift book, students described significant events that occurred in specific years, using the date on a penny as a guide.

Science

Like social studies, science offers sequential data that can be presented in a gift book. Students will enjoy putting together books on life cycles and photosynthesis. Science also abounds with categories that can be broken down into smaller pieces—like "how animals protect themselves," "seed dispersal," and "the solar system."

- Natural phenomena
- Plant and animal kingdoms
- Art in science
- "What Makes a Scientist" books
- Wonders of nature
- Leaf prints
- Animal tracks
- Identification books (birds, rocks, leaves, seeds, trees)
- Keepsake books for pictures or illustration of scientific phenomena

Mathematics

The combination of literature and mathematics is a recent and interesting development. Many math concepts are embedded in stories, and they likewise can be presented in an accordionlike fashion. Here are a few ideas:

- Retellings of math literature
- Original math stories
- Descriptions of math concepts (money, math in our lives, tangrams, geometric shapes)
- Multiplication-facts reference guide
- Geometric shapes guide

Music

Today, songs have become reading material; they are often reproduced or depicted in storylike formats. Lyrics from popular songs can be transcribed and illustrated in a personalized, gift accordion book. A few starter ideas are listed below.

- Lyrics to songs
- Original songs
- Musical impressions—responding emotionally to music

Suggested Literature

MacLachlan, P. **Sarah, Plain and Tall.** HarperCollins, 1985. (LA, SS)
Responding to the story of Sarah, as she leaves her Maine home by the sea and resettles in the Midwest, seems to happen almost effortlessly with most young readers. This engaging text can be retold as a gift book and given to someone who would appreciate Sarah's life story. Students might try to capture Sarah's memories or reflections on fanlike pages of their gift accordion books. If they adopt Sarah's point of view, students might design the books as gifts for her two stepchildren.

Locker, T. & C. Christiansen. **Sky Tree: Seeing Science Through Art.** HarperCollins, 1995. (S)
Using oils, the authors depict a single tree, surrounded by an expansive sky, as it is altered by the seasons and by the rising and setting of the sun. The tranquil mood of the artwork carries over into the text, which underscores and explains the illustrations. Students could choose a tree from on, or near, the school grounds and illustrate its changes throughout the year. They could also look for other picture books that combine artistic techniques with science.

Ashabranner, B. **Always to Remember: The Story of the Vietnam Veterans Memorial.** Scholastic, 1988. (SS)
This inspiring story chronicles the building of the Vietnam War Memorial. As a response to the text, students could research the building of other memorials in Washington, D.C., throughout the United States, in their hometowns, or in the world. After gathering information and deciding on their focus, they can portray the construction of the chosen memorials (and what or who they represent) in a gift accordion book.

Moss, M. **Amelia's Notebook.** Tricycle Press, 1995. (LA, SS)
This hand-lettered book contains a nine-year-old girl's thoughts and feelings at having to move, leave her best friend, start at a new school, and deal with her older sister. Often told with humor, *Amelia's Notebook* can serve as a model for students to record their thoughts on siblings, friendships, and other aspects of growing up. Each folded page in their accordion books can contain a day's entry. With this spin on the activity, the gift book becomes a personal journal—or a gift to oneself.

Dee, R. **Two Ways to Count to Ten.** Henry Holt, 1988. (M, LA) This Liberian folktale retells a traditional tale in which King Leopold invites all the animals in his kingdom to enter a spear-throwing contest. The winner will get to marry his daughter and succeed him as king. In addition to retelling the story, students could depict other ways to get to a numeral such as 10—for instance, counting by 2s or 5s, dividing 20 by 2, and multiplying 5 times 2. Both approaches make for great gift accordion books.

Other Suggested Titles

Haskins, J. **Colin Powell: A Biography.** Scholastic, 1992. (SS)
Viorst, J. **Sad Underwear and Other Complications.** Simon & Schuster, 1995. (LA)
Cobb, M. **The Quilt-Block History of Pioneer Days.** Millbrook Press, 1995. (SS)
Stevens, J. **From Pictures to Words: A Book About Making a Book.** Holiday House, 1995. (LA)
Vierira, L. **The Ever-Living Tree: The Life and Times of a Coast Redwood.** Walker and Company, 1994. (S)

Students use Wisdom Books to communicate lessons about life, share inspiring thoughts, and offer sage advice!

Wisdom Books:

Learning from Literature

Description

Books have long been regarded as a source of knowledge. They can also provide a source of inspiration. And the recent rise in the number of inspirational books has yielded countless models for student-created adaptations. While they enjoy and learn from this creative activity, students meet characters who provide valuable advice and wisdom through their actions and dialogue. These books and the adaptations they spawn will add a rich resource to your classroom literacy program.

Materials

- A variety of inspirational books
- Writing paper, adding-machine paper, mural paper
- Poster board or oak tag
- Markers and art materials
- Binder rings, staples, or brads
- Binder machine (if available)
- Magazine pictures
- Scissors

How to Prepare

Wisdom books are a relatively easy project for you to prepare—and for students to complete. Once you begin to immerse them in this new genre, students need only know that advice can come from the characters in literature. You can help by locating and modeling appropriate actions, sayings, quotes, and passages. Ask students to write them on lengths of adding-machine paper, oak-tag strips, and sections of mural paper to make banners, and on poster board and oak tag for posters and charts. Then display the inspirational words throughout the classroom—even hung from the ceiling. You can also bind students' work into wisdom books, which is discussed below in the Publishing Tips.

Wisdom Books: Across the Curriculum

Although most wisdom books would tend to apply to language arts activities, other curricular areas can serve as models or inspiration. Science and social studies often provide instructions or bits of wisdom in order to help us perform something more successfully.

Publishing Tip

There are a variety of means to publish wisdom books. The pages can be collected and bound into a book using a binding machine; or, if one is unavailable, it can be stapled together. Additional means of publishing include other *Books Don't Have to Be Flat!* activities, such as baggie books (see page 10), stories in a can (see page 17), graduated pages (see page 31), and hung-up books (see page 71). If you choose hung-up books, the hanger can be decorated like a character, such as Winnie the Pooh, with a speech bubble available for the chosen saying, quote, or advice.

In addition to using inspirational literature, be sure to involve members of the school community as "expert" sources. To gather more wisdom, students could interview the principal, the school nurse, or the custodian, as well as residents of nursing homes and senior-citizen communities. Once the book is published, share copies with the contributors.

Language Arts

Language arts will yield a wealth of inspiration examples. There are many advice books on the market, many written for (or by) children. And the revealing and insightful comments made by fictional characters can be discussed, analyzed, and turned into entries for a wisdom book.

Wisdom Book: Young Anna, a character from *Sarah, Plain and Tall,* **provides advice to others on how to survive and live on the prairie.**

A brief list of suggestions follows.

- Quotes from characters in books offering advice
- Analyzing actions of characters to glean lessons
- Advice columns in newspapers and magazines
- "Welcome to Our School" book
- Adaptations from literature (for example, *Life's Little Instruction Book, Seussisms, Pooh's Little Instruction Book*)
- Letters of advice (to the newly elected President of the United States, to next year's fourth graders, to the student population)
- How-to books ("How to Be a Good Sport," "How to Be a Leader")

Social Studies

Much wisdom springs from history, historical figures, cultures, and so forth. Our own country was founded by people who strongly believed in simple wisdom. Many of our nation's early texts, like *Poor Richard's Almanac* and the Constitution, guided our citizens and helped them to learn and live together. Today, advice is sought and given on helping troubled nations and peoples, on running governments, and on following rules in society. Here are a few ideas for wisdom books in social studies:

- Proverbs
- Adages
- "Random Acts of Kindness" book
- How-to books (making a cultural artifact, performing a dance from another culture, getting along with one another)
- Advice or words of wisdom from historical figures and world leaders (Mother Theresa, Dr. Martin Luther King, Jr., Abraham Lincoln)
- Publications, documents, journals, diaries that contain information meant to inspire and guide

Science

While the science curriculum does not offer wisdom of the inspirational variety, much can be learned from scientists and scientific endeavors.

These ideas make for great science wisdom books:

- Advice (from an extrater-restrial point of view) to human beings on how to save Earth from pollution and eventual destruction
- Advice to (or from) scientists (paleontologists, researchers, entomologists)
- How-to books (pet care, caring for the environment, physical fitness)
- Instructions on conducting an experiment, doing an observation, writing a report

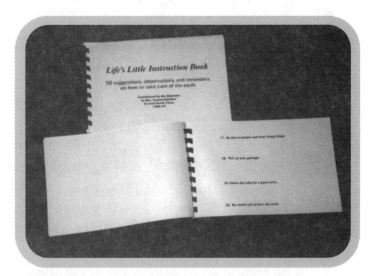

Wisdom Books can be constructed where students provide advice on how to save the earth—a perfect way to celebrate Earth Day.

Suggested Literature

Brown, J. **Wit and Wisdom from the Peanut Butter Gang.** Rutledge Hill Press, 1994. (LA)
This clever collection of advice and inspiration from children themselves can serve as models for students' own advice to their peers, younger classmates, parents, or the new principal. In addition to wisdom books and banners, their advice can appear in school or class newspapers and yearbooks or on school calendars.

Brown, J. **Life's Little Instruction Book.** Rutledge Hill Press, 1995. (LA)
Another installment in a very popular series, this book has inspired many variations and clones. After reading several pieces of Brown's advice, students can write or provide their own on a variety of subjects—for instance, advice to future sixth graders, advice to soldiers in the Civil War (through the eyes of, say, General Lee or Abraham Lincoln), and advice on saving the earth.

Milne, A. **Pooh's Little Instruction Book.** Dutton, 1995. (LA)
Here's another pint-size book filled with advice from the *Winnie the Pooh* characters. Students could compile a wisdom book based on the advice

of Milne's characters, or they might be inspired to create new animal characters for their own "Instruction Books."

Rathmann, P. **Officer Buckle and Gloria.** G.P. Putnam's and Sons, 1995. (LA, SS)
This Caldecott winner can be enjoyed simply for its excellent story line, or it can serve as a basis for the discussion of safety tips. In an inventive design idea, the story's safety tips appear on star shapes. After brainstorming other safety tips, students might draw their own shapes to enhance their wisdom bits. They can design these for display around the room or create a wisdom book on safety.

Seuss, **Dr. Seussisms: Advice from the Good Doctor.** Random House, 1996. (LA, SS, S)
The dean of children's books delivers again in this collection of advice and sage sayings from several characters that appear in Dr. Seuss's books. Seussisms offers a great model to get students started. Then, as they read other books—novels, biographies, fables—students could collect wise sayings from characters and compile them in a "Words of Wisdom" book. For a variation on the activity, students write advice on strips of paper and hang them in the classroom.

MacLachlan, P. **Sarah, Plain and Tall.** HarperCollins, 1985. (LA, SS)
Sarah gives plenty of advice to her stepchildren Caleb and Anna on how to enjoy their homeland and the things that have been given to them. Students could extract and collect this advice, or they may create additional advice that Sarah might have given the children. Another Sarah-inspired idea for a wisdom book might catalogue tips on how to adjust to life on the prairie.

Other Suggested Titles

Yolen, J. **A Sip of Aesop.** Scholastic, 1995. (LA)
Lord, S. **Garbage: The Trashiest Book You'll Ever Read.** Scholastic, 1993. (S)
Singer, M. **Twenty Ways to Lose Your Best Friend.** HarperCollins, 1990. (LA, SS)
McKissack, P. & F. McKissack. **Sojourner Truth: Ain't I a Woman?** Scholastic, 1992. (SS)

After a multicultural study of *Cinderella Around the World* students wrote postcards from their version of Cinderella.

Traveling Books:

Postcard Books and Beyond

Description

Authors use a variety of writing forms, (letters, diaries, notes, lists, postcards, and journals) to help convey their stories, messages, or information. With the traveling books activity, students learn to present information by writing in a unique way. The results will "travel" beyond the flat pages of a flat book.

Materials

- Writing materials
- Various kinds of paper
- Art supplies (crayons, markers, paints)
- Magazines, photographs, travel brochures
- Books that model writing forms

How to Prepare

This activity requires very little preparation, as students will use their regular writing supplies and art materials. Once the topic is determined, or the "book" is chosen, the students simply record their information or responses using a selected writing format such as postcards, letters, logs, or journals.

Publishing Tip

Having available a supply of pre-cut paper makes this book activity work like a snap. For example, rectangular shaped pieces of paper will serve as postcards. Pictures cut out of magazines along with photographs that students bring from home can be used for the front of the postcard, or students can illustrate the postcards themselves.

If students are simulating letters, journals, or logs, and they would like an aged look, immersing crumpled paper in a weak tea solution gives the desired effect. For these simulated journals, students might write from the point of view of a literary character or historical figure. Your young poets can compile a postcard collection of original poetry.

Traveling Books: Across the Curriculum

Across the curriculum we find various types of writing used to present information or concepts. Social studies features primary documents such as memoirs and journals in their recounts of historical figures. In language arts, authors often employ various forms of writing (for instance, letters or diaries) to develop characterization or to reveal part of the plot. The genre of historical fiction also makes frequent use of the primary-document style. Science is even beginning to incorporate more writing styles to present important facts in an unprecedented way.

Language Arts

In developing their stories, authors occasionally have their characters write. Characters may keep journals or diaries to reflect their thoughts and feelings or write letters to others to speak their mind or get what they want. Occasionally, writers will write a whole novel in the form of a letter or journal. This literary device can both simulate reality and put us smack inside the mind of a character.

Traveling Books: Postcard Books. Students wrote postcards as if they were Disney characters—Pinocchio, Snow White, Cinderella, and so forth.

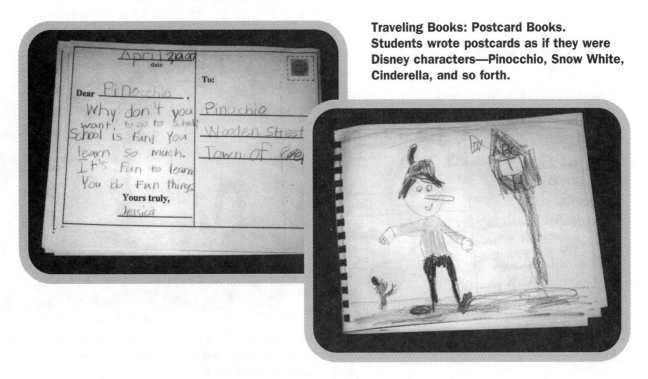

The following list of these traveling-book ideas will come in handy.

- Character studies (diary or letter from character's point of view)
- Simulated journals (from character's point of view)
- Letters or postcards from characters (to other characters, to children, or to parents in the school community)

Science

Scientific information is occasionally presented in atypical ways—for example, through postcards, diaries, or memoirs. The subjects listed below offer some interesting opportunities for your students to write from unique points of view.

- Postcards from the planets, rain forests, desert
- Diaries or logs kept by scientists or by animals (commenting on their habitat, diet, predators or prey, etc.)
- Metamorphosis ("How I Became a Butterfly, Frog, Duck, etc.")
- Animal migration ("Let me tell you about my trip...")
- Hibernation ("Here's what life underground is like...")

Social Studies

Social studies incorporates various writing forms to develop concepts and gives students insight into the feelings, motivations, and actions of people in history. Primary documents such as journals and logs have long allowed social studies students to hear history—and politics and sociology and economics—straight from the horse's mouth. Here's a list of ideas to steer students toward the educational fun of the traveling-book activity.

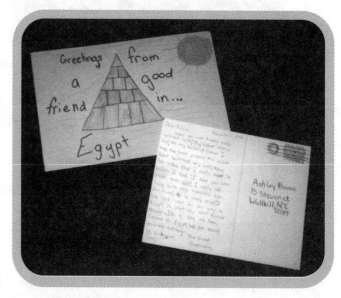

Traveling Books: Postcard Books. Postcards are sent from various characters in different versions of the Cinderella folktale.

- Diaries or letters of people in history
- Simulated journal entries of famous people (of the past or present)
- Letters from presidents, first ladies, explorers (actual or simulated)
- "If you were there" accounts
- Radio or television accounts of historic moments (Moon landing) or future events of consequence (human exploration of Mars)

Suggested Literature

Cushman, K. **The Ballad of Lucy Whipple.** Clarion Books, 1996. (Letter Writing) (SS)
A young girl, uprooted from her life on the East Coast, finds herself in a camp serving gold prospectors. She writes, often humorously, to describe her new life, her loneliness, the hardships that abound in the settling of the West, and her subsequent adjustment to her new home and situation. As they read the book, students could continue writing as Lucy, or they could choose another historical character or figure and use letter writing to both convey that person's feelings and illuminate a historical period.

Hart, T. **Antarctic Diary.** Macmillan, 1994. (Diary) (S, SS)
The harshness and beauty of life in the Antarctic is revealed in a diary format. Students could "travel" to other parts of the world and describe life, the environment, the fauna and flora, and the weather in their own travel diaries or postcards.

Leedy, L. **Postcards from Pluto: A Tour of the Solar System.** Holiday House, 1993. (Postcards) (S)
This compelling book yields information about Pluto through postcards sent from the lonely and distant planet. In responding to the text, students might undertake other "journeys": to the bottom of the ocean, to other continents, or even farther out into space. Then they could write postcards to report on their adventures.

Moss, M. **Amelia Writes Again.** Tricycle Press, 1996. (Notebook) (LA)
A ten-year-old girl draws and writes about her daily life in the journal she receives for her birthday. This endearing book gets an added charge from the humorous illustrations (supposedly drawn by the young narrator) that accompany the text. Students will also enjoy its unique design: it looks

just like the marbled notebooks found in stationery stores—and in kids' lockers. Students could use notebooks to write daily accounts of their own lives; or they might prefer to keep simulated journals from the point of view of a character in a book they are reading.

MacLachlan, P. **Sarah, Plain and Tall.** HarperCollins, 1985. (Letter Writing) (SS, LA)

Sarah communicates to both her new and old families through letter writing. Students could write additional letters from Sarah to her family or write as if they were one of Sarah's stepchildren, Caleb or Anna. Sarah may lead students to other books and characters, opening a world of viewpoints from which they can practice their writing and expand their "travels."

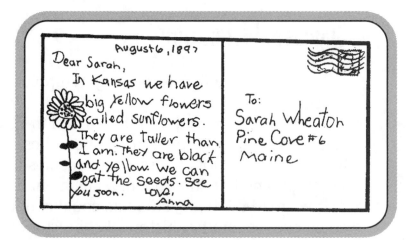

Postcard Books: *Sarah, Plain and Tall.* Anna, in her initial communications with Sarah, sends her a postcard depicting prairie sunflowers in the hopes that she can entice Sarah to come to Kansas.

George, J. **Look to the North: A Wolf Pup Diary.** HarperCollins, 1997. (Diary) (S, LA)

In this account, diary entries mark the passage of the seasons introducing events in the lives of three wolves that grow from helpless pups to participants in their small pack's hunt. This book could serve as a model for other animal or ecological reports that students may be pursuing.

George, J. **Dear Rebecca, Winter Is Here.** HarperTrophy, 1993. (Letter Writing) (S, SS, LA)

A grandmother writes to her granddaughter describing the environment where she lives. It turns out that she lives on the other side of the world, which means the seasons are the reverse of those that her granddaughter experiences. Using this book as a model, students could write letters about seasonal occurrences or other environmental issues or concerns. These letters could be sent to actual people or can be from or to characters in books.

Other Suggested Titles

Giff, P. **The Postcard Pest.** Dell, 1994. (Postcards)

James, S. **Dear Mr. Blueberry.** Macmillan, 1991. (Postcards)

Cleary, B. **Dear Mr. Henshaw.** Dell Yearling, 1979. (Letters)

Ahlberg, J. & A. Ahlberg. **The Jolly Pocket Postman.** Little, Brown, 1995. (Various writing forms)

Hackman, P. & D. Oldenburg. **Dear Mr. President: Greetings and Advice to a New Leader from His Youngest Citizens.** Avon, 1993. (Letters)

Small enough to put in a pocket, but big enough to house collections of idioms, a retelling of a math story (*The Doorbell Rang*), or a brainstorming of things that are black-and-white in color (inspired by a book), matchbook books fit the bill. Matchbook books also are perfect for highlighting student definitions of reading (as in the *Books and You: A Great Match* book).

Matchbook Books

Description

Matchbook books look like matchbooks—and that's not intended as a tongue twister. They consist of a single covering, which is folded so that the top edge inserts into the bottom fold. Because of the way this book is "bound" (at the bottom), its contents work best as single-page units of a common theme or topic, as opposed to having a sequential story line.

Materials

- Paper
- Posterboard or oak tag (optional)
- Art supplies (crayons, markers, paints)
- Stapler

How to Prepare

Determine the size of the matchbook and cut a rectangular piece of paper or posterboard accordingly. This book is intended to be small—about 4" x 3". Fold a lip (approximately ½") at the bottom edge; this will serve as the holding flap. Then fold the sheet, bringing the top edge down toward, but not all the way to, the bottom edge. This allows the top piece to fit into the flap, leaving room to bind the pages at the bottom. Cut pages to size (slightly smaller than the matchbook works best) and stack them one on top of the other. Insert the pages in the bottom flap of the matchbook and staple as close as possible to the bottom edge. The number of pages may vary but should not be too many to staple. After the books have been assembled, students can either start on the contents or decorate the covers.

Publishing Tip

The matchbook book is a favorite of children because it can be quickly assembled—and it fits into a pocket! They also hold up pretty well, too, as the fold-over cover protects the contents.

NOTE: It's best not to use too heavy a gauge of posterboard for the cover because standard staples may not sufficiently puncture it.

Matchbook Books: Across the Curriculum

These pocket-size books make perfect little homes for various kinds of work, including quick-reference materials, lists of interesting facts, and collections of wordplay fun.

Language Arts

Wordplay just seems to work in matchbook books, perhaps because their size reminds students of bubble-gum comics. Riddles, jokes, limericks, puns—all manner of wordplay fits the fun of the format. Some student-tested ideas follow:

Matchbook Books: Students' definitions of reading.

- Proverbs
- Inspirational sayings
- Parts of speech
- Autograph books
- Wordplay (palindromes, tongue twisters, knock-knock jokes)
- Color connotations (locating the use and effects of color in poetry and fiction, discussing emotions associated with certain colors)
- Vocabulary development (definitions, synonyms, antonyms)
- "What is..." books ("What is reading?", "What is a good writer?")

Science

Students love interesting information about scientific phenomena, and these matchbook books work perfectly as handy references, data compilations, and statistics lists. You can refer to this quick list to start and then add any ideas that students might have.

Matchbook Books: A matchbook book on black-and-white objects found in our environment.

- Facts about specific animals, plants, mountains, rocks, insects
- Pocket field-guide (birds, plants, flowers, shells)
- Charts and statistics on weather, natural disasters, solar eclipses

Math

Math concepts, number stories, and number facts can be spotlighted in matchbook books. Tucking away math knowledge in a little book somehow renders it less threatening to your more math-wary students. The following list can get students started on their little books.

- Word problems
- Math shapes in the real world
- Number facts (addition, multiplication, etc.)
- Math terms (dividend, improper fraction, addend, etc.)
- Ways to represent a number (for example, various equations to get to 11)
- Math in literature (*When the Doorbell Rang, Anno's Mysterious Multiplying Jar*)
- Statistics (sporting events and athletes, population cross-sections)

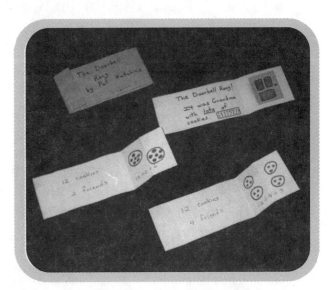

Matchbook Books: A retelling of *The Doorbell Rang.*

Social Studies

Social studies has a treasure trove of interesting facts and information that come alive in matchbook books. Topics well-suited for this small format include brief biographies, facts about our states, aspects of a culture, and exports of a nation. Here are a couple of ideas to jump-start this activity.

- Facts about states, countries, towns, rivers, etc.
- "Featuring..." books ("...the Life and Times of Lewis and Clark," "...Neil Armstrong," "...Michael Jordan")

Suggested Literature

Wexo, J. **Animal Champions.** Crestwood House, 1991. (S)
This fascinating book takes a look at unusual animals that stand out for their abilities or appearance. Working with the text and perhaps extending it with further research of particular animals, students can use the matchbook format to create their own books on animal champions. They might also apply their research to making matchbook books devoted to one animal.

Parish, P. **Teach Us, Amelia Bedelia.** Scholastic, 1977. (LA)
Amelia, unique and irrepressible, interprets the English language in a humorously unconventional way. Amelia Bedelia books are a wonderful way to learn about and enjoy figurative language. Students can find examples of figurative language in other books (for example, work by Martin Terban), in magazines, and in everyday speech. Then they can record these in matchbook books and accent the text with illustrations.

Tildes, P. **Animals: Black and White.** Charlesbridge, 1996. (S, SS, LA)
One page of this book presents information that serves as a clue to the identity of a particular black-and-white animal; the next page reveals the name of the animal. Students can find examples of black-and-white objects in their everyday lives—like dominoes, newspapers, skunks, and dice—and create a Black-and-White Matchbook Book. Other color explorations in the realms of nature and with man-made objects could also be conducted.

Krull, K. **Wish You Were Here: Emily's Guide to the 50 States.** Doubleday, 1997. (SS, LA)
As Emily and her grandmother travel throughout the United States, they gather and impart key information about each state. Students might devote an entire matchbook book to a state, a county, or a town. They could collect information similar to that amassed by Emily and her grandmother and record it in charts or statistics.

The hanger book retellings depicted here are from several versions of the popular story, *Cinderella* (*The Egyptian Cinderella, The Rough Faced Girl,* and the well-known version of Cinderella).

Hung-Up on Books

Description

Unlike most books, which you have to hold in order to read, these books are simply hung up around the classroom. You can use hooks or clothes-lines. You can hang them from chairs or ceilings. You can use any method that will result (safely) in a hung-up book! A wire hanger forms the spine—it's the skeleton of the book. From there, students transform the hangers into characters: the head of the character on the hook, the shoulders or arms (or wings or flippers) on the frame. In addition to depicting characters, hung-up books offer an interesting means of portraying historical figures—or even the children themselves. After a unit of study, students can create a gallery of important people to be hung around the room; or, in a leap back from social studies to the classroom, students can create hanger self-portraits.

Whatever the choice of content, the portrayed figure (student, character, or historical figure) should be described on an attached piece of paper, which hangs from the bottom of the frame. Student portraits are especially appropriate for Back-to-School Nights, whereas characterization works well for both language arts and social studies. The created figures do not have to be realistic or human—animals and imaginary beings make great subjects, too. For a variation, use hangers as writing displays, on which students' prefolded stories, poems, and reports are draped and exhibited around the room.

Materials

- Wire hangers
- Assorted art materials (crayons, colored pencils, markers, paint, brushes)
- Construction paper (various colors)
- Small paper plates (or posterboard)
- Fabric, trim, sequins, feathers, yarn
- Scissors, art knife, safety scissors
- Glue, tape

How to Prepare

The hung-up books activity is easy to prepare. In fact, students do almost all the work. First, acquire a bunch of wire hangers (see Publishing Tip on next page). Then collect in one place the materials for creating and decorating the portraits. Small paper plates make great heads, but if plates are unavailable, you can pre-cut posterboard circles. Depending on the needs of your class, you might want to affix some heads (and maybe shoulders) to hangers to get students started. Ask students to help you prepare by folding sheets of construction paper in half. These will be draped over the bottom of the hanger frame and will showcase students' writing—whether it accompanies the portraits or hangs on its own.

Hung-Up on Books: Across the Curriculum

Hanger creations deliver a dose of delight to social studies, science, and language arts. Instead of merely reporting on or discussing historical figures, literary characters, and groundbreaking scientists, students can construct the lesson in a hung-up book. Regardless of the curricular area, students will have fun as they learn to get hung-up on books.

Social Studies

Studying about famous people from the past and present constitutes an important part of the social studies curriculum. The results of these studies can be hung-up around the room—a takeoff, perhaps, on a wax museum. Career exploration can likewise be represented at a Career Fair, with hung-up examples of various careers. Here are some examples of these topics.

- Career opportunities (veterinarian, movie director, architect)
- Well-known athletes, first ladies, astronauts, presidents, explorers

Science

Reports on animals make vibrant hung-up books. Students can create animal figures and attach the relevant information (on paper draped from the bottom of the hanger frame) to the body of the animal. These topics are student-tested winners:

- Animals from around the world
- Scientists (careers—biologist, geologist, entomologist—or important scientists—Marie Curie, Jonas Salk, George Washington Carver)

Language Arts

Imagine a gallery of book characters hanging around the room. What a unique way to discuss characterization! Of course, hanger portraits need not be limited to literature selections. Students can also cast an eye inward to render self-portraits. (And let's not forget you, the teacher!)

Hung-Up on Books: *Sarah, Plain and Tall.* Sarah introduces herself in this hung-up on books format *(right)*.

Hung-Up on Characters: Storybook characters and a student's autobiography are hung around the room *(below)*.

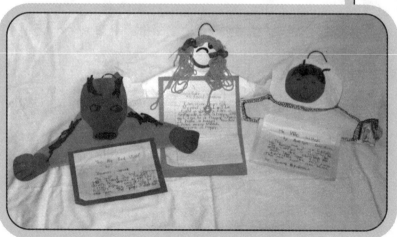

The list below fleshes out a couple of ideas.

- Self-portraits (with written autobiographies attached)
- Character portraits with characterizations (from stories, myths, folktales—for example, the many cultural variants of Cinderella)

Suggested Literature

Climo, S. **The Egyptian Cinderella.** HarperCollins, 1989. (LA, SS)
In this tale, Rhodopis, a slave girl, eventually weds the Pharaoh and becomes queen. Some students might want to portray Rhodopis with a hanger portrait, accompanied by brief text that highlights her story. Others may create hung-up books about other Cinderella stories from around the world.

Bedik, S. **Thomas Edison: Great American Inventor.** Scholastic, 1995. (SS, S, LA)
In this interesting and accessible biography, the great inventor comes alive. A group of students could create a Thomas Edison hang-up book, which could be displayed along with other students' hanger work in a class museum devoted to famous scientists. Accompanying the Edison hanger-portrait could be a mobile (also a hanger-work) showing illustrations of his inventions.

Wexo, J. **Elephant Zoobook.** Wildlife Education, 1986. (S)
Part of an effective and popular series, this edition provides information, illustrations, and photographs about the life and habits of elephants. Students may wish to make elephant hanger-books and attach key data and fascinating facts to the elephant's body. Remember that other animals are fair game, too!

George, J. **My Side of the Mountain.** Viking, 1959. (S, LA)
An enduring classic, this story transports us to the adventurous days of a young boy in the Catskill Mountains. All the characters, including the bird, can become hanger representations. Students might attach the actions and thoughts of the characters to the hung-up body. Other hanger work might show information that pertains to survival in the mountains.

MacLachlan, P. **Sarah, Plain and Tall.** HarperCollins, 1985. (LA, SS)
Any of the characters in this honest and inspiring book would make
worthwhile subjects for hanger portraits. Information attached to the
bodies may express the character's feelings or thoughts or describe what
it's like to live on the prairie. Suggest to students that they present their
prairie information from a social studies perspective.

Other Suggested Titles

Martin, R. **The Rough-Face Girl.** Scholastic, 1992. (a Cinderella story)
     (LA, SS)
DePaola, T. **Strega Nona.** Scholastic, 1975. (LA)
McGovern, A. **The Secret Soldier: The Story of Deborah Sampson.**
     Scholastic, 1975. (SS)
Brandt, K. **Marie Curie: Brave Scientist.** Troll, 1983. (SS, S)
Cole, J. **The Magic School Bus Lost in the Solar System.** Scholastic,
     1991. (SS)

Children Around the World:
A Model Unit for Using
Books Don't Have to Be Flat!
Activities

Overview

How can you apply the activities in this book to an ongoing unit of study? That's the most important question we've been asked. In response, we have selected a global theme: Children Around the World. This theme's adaptability and relevance make it a practical tool in avoiding flatness in your students' education. But that's not the only reason it works. Undertaking themes that identify and celebrate cultural diversity increases understanding and respect across cultures. It helps students discover similarities and differences between themselves and other children around the world. By learning about various cultures, students will be able to see the world through another's eyes.

When planning any thematic unit, it's important to think about the intended learning objectives. How do the objectives reinforce the theme— and vice versa? Whether the objectives stem from a specific content area, like science or social studies, or fall under broader categories in the language arts, the theme of Children Around the World will reinforce curricular goals. As a teacher, you know that meeting content-specific objectives depends on developing the fundamental skills of language arts: reading, writing, listening, and speaking. These skills provide the means to acquire and express the knowledge that results from completing a unit of study. In this sample unit, Children Around the World, we offer objectives that not only reinforce the theme but that transport children throughout an animated curriculum that will leave the flat world behind!

◢ Objectives for Unit

- Familiarity with a variety of cultures
- Recognition of the similarities and differences among cultures throughout the world
- Development of respect for the customs, traditions, and values of other cultures
- Ability to identify the similarities and differences among cultures depicted in literature
- Development of map skills in locating the countries studied in the unit
- Appreciation for a variety of literary genres

In addition to these objectives, this unit offers a way to teach language arts while encouraging children to express what they learn in a variety of ways. As they "travel" the world, your students will visit children in far-away places, learning about their surroundings, customs, foods, arts, and so on. They'll have the opportunity to read, write, and research—and to demonstrate their knowledge in various ways throughout their journey. The unit's literature and activities will help students develop an under-standing and appreciation of other cultures and ways of life. As a result, they can begin to face complex, global issues with both sensitivity and honesty. In exploring this theme, your students will learn that it is "a small world after all." (See the semantic map for Children Around the World on the next page.)

Beginning the Journey

Without even leaving the classroom, students can launch into travel and adventure by taking a literature voyage around the world. To introduce the adventure, you can read *The Fantastic Flying Journey* by Gerald Durrell. This magical book, subtitled "An Adventure in Natural History," recounts the travel adventures of the eccentric Uncle Lancelot and his great-niece and great-nephew. These world travelers undertake in a hot-air balloon an epic voyage to many exotic places. While your students follow the adventures of Uncle Lancelot and his crew, the classroom journey can begin!

Artifact Books
Decorate boxes for a collection of objects or pictures that reflect settings, culture, clothing, characters, etc. Examples: *Sadaka and a Thousand Paper Cranes* (fan, green tea, Japanese flag), *The Egypt Game* (mazes, a crown, sand, jewelry)

Postcard Books
Students write postcards from characters. The illustrations are to reflect the locations they write from. Examples: *Postcards from Outer Space, The Stringbean's Trip to the Shining Sea*

Children Around the World

Wisdom Books
Write an advice book to prepare others for a trip around the world. Examples: *Life's Little Instruction Book, My Wish for Tomorrow*

Stories in a Can Linear Books
Draw a story map mural for a journey book. Examples: *The Fantastic Flying Journey, Journey to Jo'burg*

Hung-Up on Books
Use hangers as body frames to illustrate characters from literature. Examples: *Rainbow Books, Heidi*

Box Books
Using an accordion folded format, retell a story. Summarize plot, characters, setting, and ending. Examples: *Heidi, The Magic Tree*

Gift Books
Make a "photo album" gift book using magazine pictures of places "visited" through literature. Examples: *Learning to Swim in Swaziland, Eskimo Boy*

Matchbook Books
Retell folktales, legends, fairy tales or fables. Examples: *Legend of the Indian Paintbrush, The Cowtail Switch and Other West African Stories*

Graduated-Pages Books
Use pages to classify information from other cultures (symbols, language, costume). Examples: *The Egypt Game, Rainbow Kid*

Baggie Books
Begin a collection of rhymes and games from around the world. Examples: *String Games Around the World, Anna Banana-101 Jump Rope Rhymes*

The armchair adventure begins in your students' hometown, where certain classroom preparations have to be completed prior to leaving. Although we can travel the continents by various means of transportation, this trip draws inspiration from *The Fantastic Flying Journey.* Your class will be going via hot-air balloon! First, students need to design their balloon and equip it with needed supplies such as food, clothing, tools, recording instruments, and maps. Ask them to brainstorm a list of items essential for the trip, how these items should be stored, and other issues to consider before departing. Students can compile their ideas in an instruction booklet.

After designing and equipping the balloon, students choose a destination; or you introduce them to the country or area to be visited. Along with students, locate the country on a map. Then they should plot the number of miles they'll be traveling. Now that they've battened down the hatches, it's time for travel diaries—which become students' passports to learning about the areas they'll visit. Graduated-pages books can serve as diaries, with one country per page or per whole book. In the latter case, each page may have information on a single topic: clothing, weather, foods, favorite activities, the arts, celebrations, and so forth. These diaries become special places for students to keep track of events on the tour, the books they read, and their thoughts and ideas about the literature and their imaginary adventures.

Traveling the World

Along with daily reading of *The Fantastic Flying Journey,* you might like to share these other books: *This Is the Way We Go to School* and *We Are Alike...We Are Different.* Both of these texts give students an opportunity to discuss, consider, and compare the ways in which people throughout the world are alike and different. You might also display other books that feature world travel. Students can use this extra material for independent reading and research, read-alouds, and guided reading. And students should be encouraged to bring in additional books about—and artifacts or products from—the countries to be visited. Keep these things in a special box or section of the classroom— or let the classroom evolve into a living and growing museum!

Culturally diverse literature shows us the uniqueness of individual cultures and the universality of all cultures (Sims Bishop, 1992). It reveals that humankind shares common experiences, while retaining distinctive cultural traditions. As a fun exercise, students compare their own community and traditions with those of the countries they visit. Then they can compile and display their observations in "Children Around the World" baggie books. Students could also construct and discuss Venn diagrams and then store them in their baggie books. Through these selections, with their authentic images from other cultures, children experience an important truth: while all cultures are distinct and different, people share such universal needs as food, shelter, clothing, love, acceptance, belonging, family, and friends. (Cullinan & Galda, 1994)

Using Literature Along the Way

In addition to reading books about a people and their nation, a country's folklore should also be explored through folktales, which offer insights into a cultural group's experiences, dreams, and values. Like a cultural mirror, folktales reflect the beliefs, rituals, and music of a people's heritage. For each destination, the class can experience some of the wondrous literature that belongs to that culture—from the Anansi tales of Africa to the dragon tales in New Zealand to the Baba Yaga tales of Russia. Children can re-create these in story-in-a-can books or write their own versions in box stories.

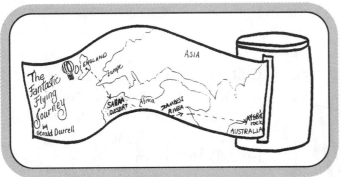

Of course, literature should also be tapped in the researching of the visited countries and regions. So, in addition to stories, folklore, poetry, and the like, you'll want to make available to students nonfiction text—magazines, atlases, encyclopedias, dictionaries, almanacs, and CD-ROMs. Students might also collect or send away for brochures, publications, and travel guides, which also become part of the reading materials for this theme.

Recording the Trip Through Writing

Writing activities can be inspired by books, current events, and worthwhile TV programs; or they may just spring from the interests of the students themselves. The following is a brief sampling of writing activities:

- Writing a diary from the point of view of a character in the literature
- Writing original poems or stories patterned after the literature of the country (for example, Anansi stories from Africa or haiku poetry from Japan)
- Writing travel-magazine or newspaper articles about a visited place (with descriptions of scenic spots, adventure stories, advertisements for native products, etc.)
- Sending postcards from characters (at top right is an example of a postcard sent by Emma on her trip around the world in *The Fantastic Flying Journey*)
- Conducting research and writing reports about the places or about the contributions of people who live or lived there
- Introducing a pen-pal program, which can be conducted through the regular mail or by e-mail. NOTE: Gift books (bottom right) can be sent to pen pals.

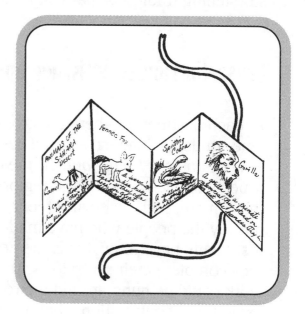

Arts from Around the World

No trip to a foreign land would be complete without experiencing the music, dance, and theater of the country. During your students' "visit" to each country, they might view museum exhibits and attend the ballet, folk dances, and circuses—with the help of literature, of course! Every country will provide unique cultural offerings that will enrich and entertain the class.

To incorporate art into the destinations, students can make murals, undertake projects, and illustrate their books, brochures, and reports. In addition, you can expose them to the art of particular countries. They might try their hands at art projects like *pysanky,* or egg-decorating (Ukraine), shadow-puppet making (Java and China), calligraphy (Japan), carving (the Maori of New Zealand), and kite-making (China). Each country has a cultural heritage that will widen the artistic horizons of the children.

While traveling throughout the world, opportunities also abound for dramatic work. Students can choose their favorite folktales to dramatize, or they could rewrite one of the tales and present it as a Readers Theater production. Many countries—like China, Ghana, and Colombia—have rich storytelling traditions that will reinforce the unit theme.

Cross-Curricular Activities and the World Journey

At each destination, there are cross-curricular possibilities, depending on time, students' interest, and the destinations themselves. Like the travelers in *The Fantastic Flying Journey,* the class can explore the natural-history aspects of each country and region, learning about the flora and fauna, the climate, and the environment, or they may want to learn about and portray the people who have made a difference to the countries they visit. If students have time, this is the perfect place for hanger books. After they complete their portraits (with accompanying biography bodies), their work could be hung around the room. Students might then go on to explore the contributions that many countries have made to humanity—

for instance, the invention of paper by the Chinese. You might start a class discussion on the implications of these contributions and the role they play in our own lives. The results of this dialogue can produce interesting results that lead to active-learning ideas: For example, children could undertake a "No Paper Day," or they could note in their journals each time they use paper (and how much) during the course of a day.

Let's not forget physical education. Each country enjoys its own games and sporting events, and children should be introduced and exposed to the many different physical activities that occupy children around the world. Hopscotch, table tennis, gymnastics, jump-rope, soccer, and kick-bag are just some of the games that work up a sweat on kids all over the world. Maybe your students could research—and play—some more!

Homeward Bound

What makes a good ending? Screenwriters aren't the only ones who face that question. Well, we think we have a few good ideas to wrap up the theme of Children Around the World. The class can create a museum to display creations and products that resulted from the thematic study. Once the museum is up and running, students should review the literature they read for this unit. As they do, they can collect quotes from fictional characters and from the actual people who live or have lived in these countries. Students write these world-travel reminders on adding-machine paper (or precut paper strips) and then hang them up or collect them in books—which of course don't have to be flat!

Now this idea can extend to a beautiful celebration: Students become museum curators and invite others to the opening of a special exhibit. The opening can feature foods from around the world, along with music from other lands playing in the background. If the study concludes during an Olympics year, an Olympic festival and games would make a great culminating project. Matchbook books can contain information about the various Olympic events.

To tie up Children Around the World, students can recall their travels in stories in a can or piece together the entire journey by creating a baggie-book quilt, each square showing something worthy of remembering from their Fantastic Journey Around the World!

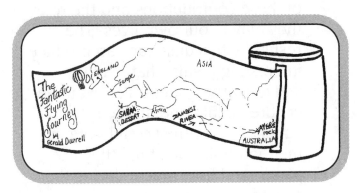

Books for "Children Around the World"

Baer, E. **This Is the Way We Go to School: A Book About Children Around the World.** New York: Scholastic, 1990.

Cheltenham Elementary School Kindergartners. **We Are All Alike... We Are All Different.** New York: Scholastic, 1991.

Choi, S. **Year of Impossible Goodbyes.** Boston: Houghton Mifflin, 1991.

Corwin, J. **Harvest Festivals Around the World.** Parsippany, NJ: Silver Burdett, 1996.

Cowen-Fletcher, J. **It Takes a Village.** New York: Scholastic, 1994.

Daly, N. **Not So Fast Songololo.** New York: Puffin Books, 1985.

Day, N. **The Lion's Whiskers: An Ethiopian Folktale.** New York: Scholastic, 1995.

DePaola, T. **Days of the Blackbird: A Tale of Northern Italy.** New York: Putnam, 1997.

Dooley, N. **Everybody Cooks Rice.** Minneapolis, MN: Carolrhoda Books, 1991.

Dorros, A. **This Is My House.** New York: Scholastic, 1992.

Durrell, G. **The Fantastic Flying Journey.** New York: Simon & Schuster, 1987.

Feldman, E. **Birthdays and Celebrations Around the World.** Watertown, MA: Bridgewater Books, 1996.

Fernandez, M. **Rainbow Kids.** Miami, FL.: DDl Books, 1995.

Gerberg, M. **Geographunny: A Book of Global Riddles.** New York: Clarion, 1991.

Gray, N. **A Country Far Away.** New York: Orchard Books, 1988.

Grifalconi, A. **The Village of Round and Square Houses.** Boston: Little, Brown and Company, 1986.

Haskins, J. **Count Your Way Through Germany.** Minneapolis, MN: Carolrhoda Books, 1990.

Heide, F. & Gilliland, J. **The Day of Ahmed's Secret.** New York: Lothrop, Lee, & Shepard, 1990.

Heide, F. & Gilliland, J. **Sami and the Time of the Troubles.** New York: Clarion, 1992.

Hocking, J. **It's One World.** Victoria, Australia: Five Mile Press, 1989.

Hru, D. **Joshua's Masai Mask.** New York: Lee & Low Books, 1993.

Joosee, B. **Mama, Do You Love Me?** New York: Scholastic, 1991.

Kalman, B. **Homes Around the World.** New York: Crabtree Publishing Co., 1994.

Kendall, R. **Eskimo Boy: Life in an Inuqiaq Eskimo Village.** New York: Scholastic, 1992.

Klamath County YMCA Family Preschool. **The Land of Many Colors.** New York: Scholastic, 1993.

Kroll, V. **Masai and I.** New York: Four Winds Press, 1992.

Krupp, R. **Let's Go Traveling.** New York: Morrow Junior Books, 1992.

Lankford, M. **Hopscotch Around the World.** New York: Morrow, 1992.

Lewin, T. **Amazon Boy.** New York: Macmillan, 1993.

London, J. **Ali: Child of the Desert.** Lothrop, Lee, & Shepard, 1997.

Morris, A. **Bread, Bread, Bread.** New York: A Mulberry Paperback Book, 1989.

Morris, A. **On the Go.** New York: Scholastic, 1990.

Naidoo, B. **Journey to Jo'burg.** New York: HarperCollins, 1988.

Orlando, L. **The Multicultural Game Book.** New York: Scholastic, 1993.

Pellegrini, N. **Families are Different.** New York: Scholastic, 1991.

Polon, L. & Cantwell, A. **The Whole Earth Holiday Book.** Glenview, IL: Good Year Books, 1983.

Priceman, M. **How to Make an Apple Pie and See the World.** New York: Dragonfly Books, 1994.

Shea, P. **The Whispering Cloth: A Refugee's Story.** Honesdale, PA: Boyds Mill Press, 1995.

Cinderella Stories

Brown, M. **Cinderella.** New York: Aladdin Books, 1954.

Climo, S. **The Egyptian Cinderella.** New York: Thomas Y. Crowell, 1989.

Climo, S. **The Korean Cinderella.** New York: HarperCollins, 1993.

Climo, S. **The Irish Cinderlad.** New York: HarperCollins, 1996.

Cohlene, T. **Little Firefly: An Algonquian Legend.** Mahwah, New Jersey: Watermill Press, 1990.

Cole, B. **Princess Smartypants.** New York: G.P. Putnam's Sons, 1986.

Cole, B. **Prince Cinders.** New York: G.P. Putnam's Sons, 1987.

Compton, J. (1994). **Ashpet: An Appalachian Tale.** New York: Holiday House.

Cox, M. **Three Hundred and Forty-five Variants of Cinderella, Catskin, and Cap o'Rushes, Abstracted and Tabulated.** London: David Nutt, 1983.

Delamare, D. **Cinderella.** New York: Simon & Schuster, 1993.

Disney, W. **Cinderella.** New York: Scholastic, 1987.

Edens, C. **The Three Princesses—Cinderella, Sleeping Beauty, and Snow White.** New York: Atheneum, 1991.

Edwards, H. **Computerella.** Crystal Lake: Illinois: Rigby Education, 1992.

Ehrlich, A. **Cinderella.** New York: Dial, 1985.

Elwell, P. **Cinderella.** Chicago, Illinois: A Calico Book, 1988.

Evans, C. **Cinderella.** London: Chancellor Press, 1972.

Galdone, P. **Cinderella.** New York: McGraw-Hill, 1978.

Granowsky, A. **Cinderella: A Classic Tale** and **That Awful Cinderella.** Austin, Texas: Steck-Vaughn Point of View Series, 1993.

Goode, D. **Cinderella.** New York: Alfred A. Knopf, 1988.

Hooks, W. **Moss gown.** Boxton: Houghton Mifflin, 1987.

Huck, C. **Princess Furball.** New York: Greenwillow Books, 1989.

Jacobs, J. **Tattercoats.** New York: G.P. Putnam's Sons, 1989.

Karlin, B. **Cinderella.** New York: Trumpet, 1989.

Jackson, E. **Cinder-Edna.** New York: Lothrop, 1994.

Louie, Ai-Long. **Yeh-Shen: A Cinderella Story from China.** New York: Philomel, 1982.

Martin, R. & Shannon, D. **The Rough-face Girl.** New York: G. P. Putnam's Sons, 1992.

McKissack, P. & McKissack, F. **Cinderella.** Chicago, Illinois: Children's Press, 1985.

Mehta, L. **The Enchanted Anklet.** Toronto, Canada: Lilmur Publishing, 1985.

Melmed, L. **Prince Nautilus.** New York: Lothrop, Lee & Shepard, 1994.

Minters, F. **Cinder-Elly.** New York: Viking, 1994.

Myers, B. **Sidney Rella and the Glass Sneaker.** New York: Macmillan, 1985.

Onyefulu, O. **Chinye.** New York: Viking, 1994.

Perlman, J. **Cinderella Penguin.** New York: Puffin Books, 1992.

Perrault, C. **Cinderella.** New York: Dial Books for Young Readers, 1985.

San Jose, C. & Santini, D. **Cinderella.** Honesdale, Pennsylvania: Boyds Mills Press, 1994.

San Souci, R. **The Talking Eggs.** New York: Dial Books for Young Readers, 1989.

San Souci, R. **Sootface: An Ojibwa Cinderella Story.** New York: Doubleday, 1994.

Shorto, R. **Cinderella** and **Cinderella: The Untold Story.** New York: Carol Publishing Company, 1990.

Sierra, J. **Cinderella.** Phoenix, Arizona: The Oryx Press, 1992.

Steptoe, J. **Mufaro's Beautiful Daughters: An African tale.** New York: Lothrop, Lee & Shepard, 1987.

Winthrop, E. **Vasilissa the Beautiful.** New York: HarperCollins, 1991.

Wright, K. **Tigerella.** New York: Scholastic, 1994.

Yorinks, A. **Ugh.** New York: Farrar, Straus, Giroux, 1990.

Professional Bibliography

Armstrong, T. **Multiple Intelligences in the Classroom.** Alexandria, VA.: Association for Supervision and Curriculum Development, 1994.

Braddon, K. **Math Through Children's Literature: Making the NCTM Standards Come Alive.** Englewood, Colorado: Teacher Ideas Press, 1993.

Bromley, K. **Webbing with Literature: Creating Story Maps with Children's Books.** Boston: Allyn & Bacon, 1996.

Cullinan, B. & Galda, L. **Literature and the Child.** Orlando, FL: Harcourt Brace, 1994.

Gardner, H. **Frames of Mind: The Theory of Multiple Intelligences.** New York: Basic Books, 1983.

Johnson, P. **Literacy Through the Book Arts.** Portsmouth, NH: Heinemann, 1993.

McCarthy, T. **Multicultural Fables and Fairy Tales.** New York: Scholastic, 1993.

Miller, W. **U.S. History Through Children's Literature.** Englewood, Colorado: Teacher Ideas Press, 1997.

Milord, S. **Tales Alive.** New York: Scholastic, 1995.

Pike, K., Compain, R., & Mumper, J. **New Connections: An Integrated Approach to Literacy.** New York: Longman, 1997.

Short, K. **Literature as a Way of Knowing.** York, Maine: Stenhouse, 1997.

Walsh, N. **Making Books Across the Curriculum.** New York: Scholastic, 1994.

Walsh, N. **Easy Bookmaking: Thematic Pop-Ups, Cards and Shape Books.** New York: Scholastic, 1996.

Planning Sheet for *Books Don't Have to Be Flat!* Activities

Books Don't Have to Be Flat! Activity

_____

Literature Selection

_____

Curricular Areas

_____   _____
_____   _____

Multiple Intelligences

_____   _____
_____   _____
_____   _____

Materials Needed

_____   _____
_____   _____
_____   _____

Method

_____
_____
_____
_____

Evaluation

_____
_____
_____
_____

Assessment Rubric for *Books Don't Have to Be Flat!* Activities

	4 Exemplary	3 Proficient	2 Developing	1 Beginning
Accuracy of Information	Excellent topic development. Accurate facts. Excellent examples.	Essential information is included. Topic adequately developed.	Most information is accurate. Fair organization of topic. Few examples.	Information is scant or wrong. Topic poorly developed or organized.
Organization of Ideas	Ideas and information are well organized and supported by excellent details and examples.	Ideas are explained well and supported by good examples and reasons.	Ideas are explained adequately with some reasons and examples.	Few details or reasons are used to explain ideas.
Use of Materials	Overall appearance is excellent. Extra care is shown in using a variety of materials.	Appearance is good. Some care is shown in using a variety of materials.	Appearance is adequate. A lack of concern is shown in use of materials.	Appearance of project is not neat. Use of materials is inadequate.
Mechanics (Spelling, Grammar, Punctuation, Capitalization)	Uses correct mechanics consistently.	Uses correct mechanics most of the time.	Uses correct mechanics some of the time.	Uses mechanics marginally. Frequent errors are made.
Presentation of Activity/ Project; Sharing	Presentation excellent. Able to answer any questions.	Presentation good. Able to answer most questions.	Presentation fair. Able to answer some questions.	Presentation poor. Unable to answer questions.

Person Evaluating Project
____ Self
____ Classmate
____ Teacher

Scores by Category
____ Accuracy of Information
____ Organization of ideas
____ Use of Materials
____ Mechanics
____ Presentation

Self-Assessment of *Books Don't Have to Be Flat!* Activities

Evaluate how you did on your project by using the following scale:

Did a great job!
(I did extra work on the project.)
Did well!
(I fulfilled the requirements for the project.)
Almost did it!
(I was close, but I really didn't meet the requirements.)
Not quite.
(I did not meet the requirements this time.)

Circle one rating and be sure to explain why you earned the rating you chose.

1. I did the required preparation and research for the project.

    Did a great job!   **Did well!**   **Almost did it!**   **Not quite.**

    Explain _____

    _____

2. My project has all the required parts.

    Did a great job!   **Did well!**   **Almost did it!**   **Not quite.**

    Explain _____

    _____

3. The information I gave was accurate and organized.

    Did a great job!   **Did well!**   **Almost did it!**   **Not quite.**

    Explain _____

    _____

4. I was creative in my project.

   Did a great job!   **Did well!**   **Almost did it!**   **Not quite.**

   Explain_____

   _____

5. I remembered to use correct spelling, punctuation, and capitalization.

   Did a great job!   **Did well!**   **Almost did it!**   **Not quite.**

   Explain _____

   _____

The best thing about my project is _____

   _____

   _____.

If I could do this project over, I would _____

   _____

   _____.

Things I learned by doing this project were _____

   _____

   _____.

Student: _____ Date: _____